United States Department of the Interior

Region South of and Adjoining Yellowstone National Park

Letter from the Secretary of the Interior

United States Department of the Interior

Region South of and Adjoining Yellowstone National Park
Letter from the Secretary of the Interior

ISBN/EAN: 9783337173142

Printed in Europe, USA, Canada, Australia, Japan

Cover: Foto ©ninafisch / pixelio.de

More available books at **www.hansebooks.com**

REGION SOUTH OF AND ADJOINING YELLOWSTONE NATIONAL PARK.

LETTER

FROM

THE SECRETARY OF THE INTERIOR,

TRANSMITTING,

IN RESPONSE TO RESOLUTION OF THE SENATE OF DECEMBER 6, 1898, COPY OF A REPORT FROM THE DIRECTOR OF THE GEOLOGICAL SURVEY, GIVING DETAILED INFORMATION TOUCHING THE REGION SOUTH OF AND ADJOINING THE YELLOWSTONE NATIONAL PARK, AND ALSO EXCERPTS FROM THE REPORT OF THE SECRETARY OF THE INTERIOR FOR THE FISCAL YEAR ENDED JUNE 30, 1898, UNDER THE HEAD OF THE YELLOWSTONE NATIONAL PARK, RELATIVE TO THE REGION IN QUESTION.

DECEMBER 20, 1898.—Referred to the Committee on Forest Reservations and the Protection of Game and ordered to be printed.

DEPARTMENT OF THE INTERIOR,
Washington, December 16, 1898.

SIR: I am in receipt of Senate resolution of the 6th instant—

That the Secretary of the Interior be, and is hereby, directed to send to the Senate all the information in the possession of his Department in relation to the region south of and adjoining the Yellowstone National Park; also what steps should be taken to preserve the game in the park, and whether the region south of the park should not be put under the same control as the national park, in order to prevent the extinction of the herds of large game roaming therein.

In response thereto I have the honor to transmit herewith a copy of a report from the Director of the Geological Survey, giving detailed information touching the region south of and adjoining the Yellowstone National Park, together with excerpts from the report of the Secretary of the Interior for the fiscal year ended June 30, 1898, under the head of Yellowstone National Park, relative to the region in question, and of Gifford Pinchot, upon the examination of the forest reserves (Teton Forest Reserve, p. 109), as well as from the report made to the Department May 1, 1897, by the forest committee of the National Academy of Sciences.

In regard to so much of the resolution as inquires what steps should be taken to preserve the game in the park, it may be stated that the existing law, act of May 7, 1894 (28 Stats., p. 73), for the protection of game in the Yellowstone National Park is being as rigidly enforced as the limited force (military patrol and civil scouts) at the command of the acting superintendent of the park will permit.

To afford better protection for the game therein increased appropriations for the protection and improvement of the park are needed, to the end that additional civil scouts may be employed to apprehend poachers and other depredators upon the game.

Regarding so much of the resolution as inquires whether the region south of and adjoining the Yellowstone National Park should not be put under the same control as the national park in order to prevent the extinction of the herds of wild game roaming therein, I have this to say: That region is a part of and within the jurisdiction of the State of Wyoming. The control of wild game therein falls within the exclusive jurisdiction of the State and will remain within its exclusive jurisdiction unless that region is made a part of the Yellowstone National Park by an extension of the boundaries of the latter. That such extension can be had so as to embrace this region within the exclusive jurisdiction of the United States is shown by the following reservation of authority contained in the act of July 10, 1890 (26 Stats., 222), admitting the State of Wyoming into the Union:

Provided, That nothing in this act contained shall repeal or affect any act of Congress relating to the Yellowstone National Park, or the reservation of the park as now defined, or as may be hereafter defined or extended, or the power of the United States over it; and nothing contained in this act shall interfere with the right and ownership of the United States in said park and reservation as it now is or may hereafter be defined or extended by law; but exclusive legislation, in all cases whatsoever, shall be exercised by the United States, which shall have exclusive control and jurisdiction over the same; but nothing in this proviso contained shall be construed to prevent the service within said park of civil and criminal process lawfully issued by the authority of said State: * * *

While the title to most, if not all, of the land in the region south of and adjoining the park is in the United States, it must be remembered that the ownership of the wild game found within the limits of a State rests in the State, as has been determined by several decisions of the Supreme Court of the United States, among which is the case of Ward v. Race Horse (163 U. S., 504). By the Constitution Congress is authorized to "make all needful rules and regulations respecting the territory or other property belonging to the United States," and in the exercise of this authority can regulate the disposal and use of the public lands whether situate within or without a State.

While Congress may not be able to authorize the capture or killing of game, the ownership of which is in a State, it is believed that it can prescribe how and when the public lands may be used and can restrict or altogether deny access to or entrance upon the public lands, or any of them, for the purpose of pursuing or hunting game. It seems, therefore, that there are two ways in which the General Government can effectively take action tending to preserve wild game which roams over the region south of and adjoining the park. The first of these is to include this region within the Yellowstone National Park by an extension of its boundaries, pursuant to the reservation of authority made in the act admitting the State of Wyoming into the Union; and the second is to prohibit anyone from entering or being upon the public lands in that region for the purpose of pursuing or hunting wild game.

The lands in question have heretofore been set aside by a Presidential proclamation under the act of March 3, 1891, as a forest reservation, and under the act of June 4, 1897 (30 Stat., 35), the Secretary of the Interior is authorized "to regulate their occupancy and use, and to preserve the forests therein from destruction." It has recently (November 17, 1898) been ruled by the Attorney-General that persons violating these regulations are amenable to the laws of the United States and can be punished therefor, but whether the regulations which the Secretary of the Interior is thus authorized to make are confined to those which in their nature tend to preserve and avoid destruction of the forests, and whether hunting within such reservations is injurious to the forests or tends to their destruction, are questions which have not been considered. It may, therefore, be doubtful whether, under existing legislation, the Secretary of the Interior is clothed with sufficient authority to make regulations prohibiting the pursuing or hunting of game within the region named. Thus far no attempt has been made to make such a regulation.

In the administration of this forest reservation assistance can of course be indirectly given to the State in the enforcement of its game laws, and to that end the forest superintendents, supervisors, and rangers will be instructed as a part of their duty to not only look after the preservation of the forests and their protection from fire and other depredations, but also to cooperate in every reasonable way with the State authorities in preventing the violation in the reservation of the game laws of the State.

There is also transmitted herewith, for consideration in connection with this report, a map, prepared in the office of the Director of the Geological Survey, showing the Yellowstone National Park and the abutting timber reserves, also the land entries made in the vicinity of Jacksons Lake in the Teton Forest Reserve and in the country south of the latter reservation, together with copies of the report of the acting superintendent of the Yellowstone National Park for the fiscal year ending June 30, 1898, and of the opinion of the Attorney-General dated November 17, 1898.

Very respectfully,

The PRESIDENT OF THE SENATE.

THOS. RYAN,
Acting Secretary.

DEPARTMENT OF THE INTERIOR,
UNITED STATES GEOLOGICAL SURVEY,
Washington, D. C., December 12, 1898.

SIR: I have the honor to acknowledge the receipt, by reference from the Department, of a copy of a Senate resolution adopted December 6, 1898, calling for information in relation to the region south of and adjoining the Yellowstone National Park, the resolution being in the following words:

Resolved, That the Secretary of the Interior be, and is hereby, directed to send to the Senate all the information in the possession of his Department in relation to the region south of and adjoining the Yellowstone National Park; also what steps should be taken to preserve the game in the park, and whether the region south of the park should not be put under the same control as the national park, in order to prevent the extinction of the herds of wild game roaming therein.

In conformity with the instructions contained in your indorsement, I have the honor to submit the accompanying report in duplicate.

I am, with respect,

CHAS. D. WALCOTT, *Director.*

The SECRETARY OF THE INTERIOR.

REPORT ON THE REGION SOUTH OF AND ADJOINING THE YELLOWSTONE NATIONAL PARK, WITH ESPECIAL REFERENCE TO THE PRESERVATION AND PROTECTION OF THE FORESTS AND THE GAME THEREIN.

In accordance with the instructions of the honorable the Secretary of the Interior, I visited, during the field season of 1898, the Teton Forest Reserve, and also examined the country lying to the south of that reservation. In making the examination the valley of Jackson Lake and the Snake River were followed to the Lower Gros Ventre Butte, and an ascent was made of the northern portion of the Teton Range, the Gros Ventre Range below Jackson post-office, and the higher ridges in the eastern portion of the reservation south of Buffalo River. From several main peaks practically the whole of the reservation was seen.

The Teton Reserve includes the northern portion of the Teton Range, the valley of Jackson Lake, and the mountain ranges about the head waters of Buffalo River and north of Gros Ventre River. There is very little commercial timber within this area, owing to the fact that it has been in the past persistently burned by the Indians. All over the region young pines are springing up, and in a few years there will be a heavy forest growth over a large portion, provided fires are kept out of it. At the west foot of the Teton Range, in the western portion of the reserve, there is a small area of valley land of considerable elevation— 7,000 to 8,000 feet—and in the interior of the reserve is a large valley about Jackson Lake, also greatly elevated, its elevation ranging from 6,000 to 7,000 feet. The great elevation of these areas renders them of little value for agricultural purposes, since nothing but the hardiest vegetables can be cultivated successfully, and the areas valuable for hay are limited.

Recommendations.—I would not recommend that any part of the present reserve be taken from it, unless it be a little of the valley land on the western border. Even this, under the present law, can be settled upon and taken from the reserve upon proof of its agricultural character. The same is true of the valley land in the vicinity of Black Tail Butte, on the southern edge of the reserve.

The extension of the reserve to the south is very desirable, both in order to secure natural fire limits and to provide a winter range for the elk, antelope, and deer which have their summer range in the Yellowstone National Park. Much of the region lying to the south of the reserve is mountainous, covered with a scanty growth of timber, but capable of supporting a heavy forest growth if protected from fire. The only agricultural land within a distance of 18 miles south of the present limits of the reserve is in the valley of Snake River, the Little Gros Ventre River, and the main tributaries entering into it from the east, where there is sometimes an acre or two of agricultural land. The same is true of the valley of Gros Ventre River, where there is some agricultural land for a distance of 3 miles along the east base of Black

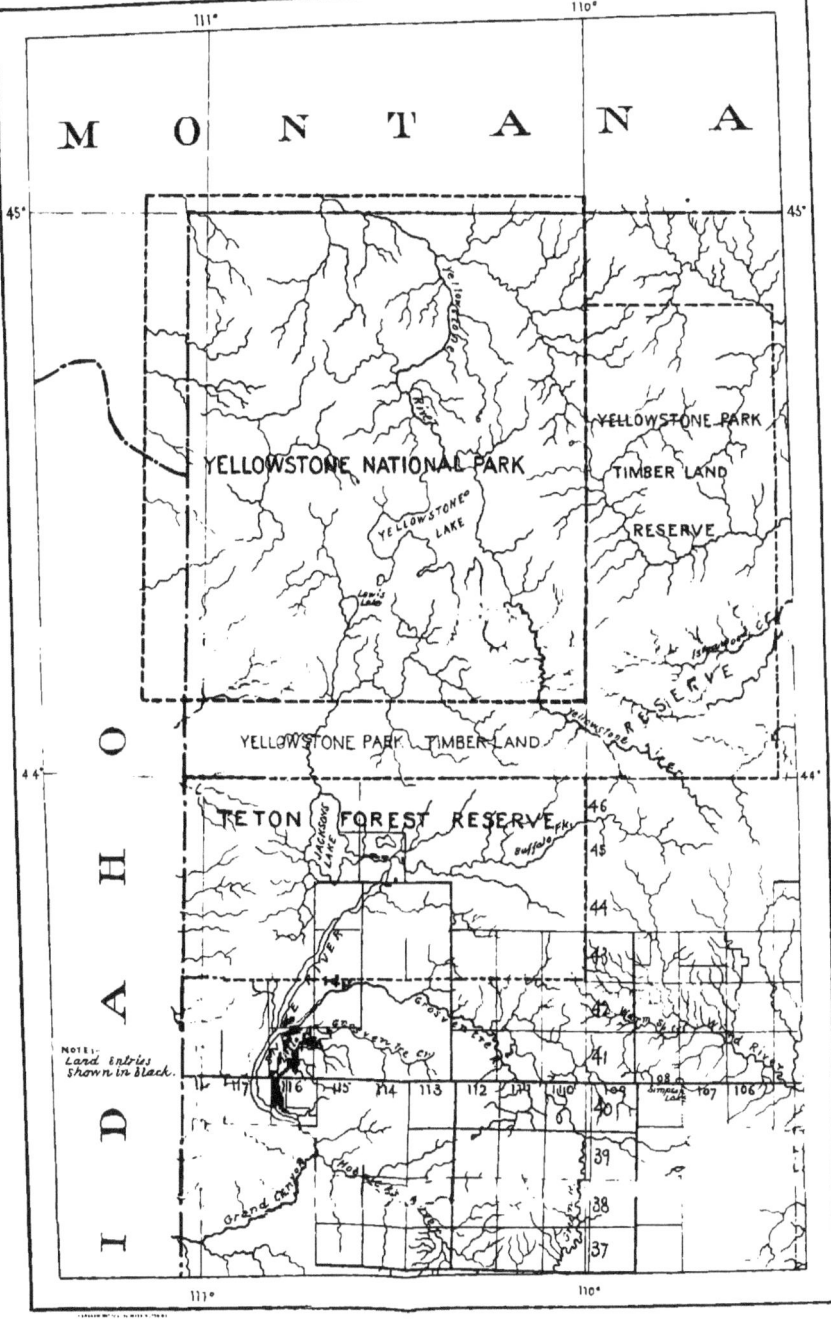

Tail or Upper Gros Ventre Butte. This is of essentially the same character as the hay lands of the lower portion of the Buffalo River Valley.

I have examined the reports of the agents sent to investigate the distribution of the forests of the Teton Reserve, and recommend that, if the region is to be kept as a forest reserve, the present eastern boundary of the Teton Reserve be extended south to the south line of township 39, and that its south line be the south boundary of township 39, running westward as far as the southwest corner of township 39, range 117 west. I also recommend that the following fractional townships, 43 and 44 north, range 118 west, be withdrawn from the Teton Reserve and restored to the public domain.

If a Teton national park is to be established I recommend that it include all of the present Teton Forest Reserve with the exception of fractional townships 43 and 44 north, in range 118 west, and that portion of the Yellowstone Timber Land Reserve lying south of the Yellowstone National Park, and also the following-described area lying south of the Teton Forest Reserve: Townships 39, 40, 41, and 42 north, in ranges 110, 111, 112, 113, and 114 west.

If such additions are made to the park it would be absolutely necessary that a strong, durable wire fence be constructed to run from the base of the Teton Range on the west to the canyon of the Gros Ventre River on the east, a distance of 18 miles, in order to prevent the game from following down the Snake River Valley into the settled districts in the Jackson Hole country.

Protection of game.—At present the game is protected in the Yellowstone National Park, and a perfect summer range is provided for it. But as winter approaches the elk, deer, moose, and antelope seek a winter range at a lower altitude or they perish. Some of the animals work off to the northeast corner of the park and winter there, but the greater number descend to the south to the Jackson Lake Basin and along to the hills and mountains to the east of the lake. Later in the fall and early in the winter heavy snow gradually drives the game south down the Snake River Valley and the mountain slopes to the east and west.

Formerly many of the elk and deer ranged as far down as 30 or 40 miles south of the Gros Ventre Butte, but with the settlement and fencing in of the bottom land, the cropping of grasses and pasturing of cattle and sheep, their winter pasture has been gradually crowded to the northward. Now, it is only a question of a few years before the winter range will all have been taken, and the game will have followed the buffalo and other large game of Colorado and other sections of the Rockies and the Sierra and Coast ranges and become extinct.

The Government is now brought face to face with the question, Shall it protect the winter range of the game which it has, at large annual expense, protected in its summer range in the Yellowstone Park? It owns and controls most of the lands of the winter range. Will it continue in this control, or will it give the lands up to the pasturage of cattle and sheep and thus exterminate the game? In September and October of the present year parties were camped on nearly every creek in the large region south of the park, waiting to shoot down the game, which they can freely do under the game laws of Wyoming, which license the hunting of large game three months each fall. Will the Government prevent the shooting of game within the Yellowstone Timber Reserve and the Teton Forest Reserve? If it does not, the rifle and shotgun will as surely exterminate the game as will the destruction of their winter pasture.

Annexation of the region south of the Yellowstone National Park to that park.—The area south of the park, extending as far as Black Tail Butte, or the southern limit of the present Teton Reserve, should either be added to the Yellowstone National Park or constituted as a separate park, to be known as the Teton National Park.

I have personally visited most of the points and regions in the United States noted for their scenery, but in my judgment there is nothing that excels in natural beauty the valley of Jackson Lake and the Teton Mountains. The Tetons are unequaled except in the higher, almost inaccessible points of the Sierra and Cascade mountains, and Jackson Lake is a beautiful sheet of water lying directly at their base. It may be more truly called the Switzerland of America than can any other spot known to me. If it were practicable to obtain railroad facilities to the foot of Jackson Lake and thus enable the tourist to see that beautiful region and then go north by stage to the Yellowstone Lake and through the park it would be the grandest trip, for one of limited extent, to be found anywhere in the world.

Settlers.—The question of the rights of settlers that are always to be found within the Teton Reserve and the region to the south can probably be adjusted under the present law, through the General Land Office, without injustice to these settlers. If not, the action of Congress can be invoked, inasmuch as the preservation of the wonderful scenery of this country and the great natural forest areas is a subject of importance to the American people.

The accompanying map shows the boundaries of the Yellowstone National Park, the Yellowstone Park Timberland Reserve, the Teton Forest Reserve, and the region lying to the south of the Teton Reserve.

Following is a report on the Teton Reserve prepared by Mr. Henry Gannett, geographer in charge of the investigation of the forests that are included within the forest reserves.

TETON RESERVE.

[By Henry Gannett, geographer, from notes by Dr. T. S. Brandegee.]

LIMITS.

This reserve is situated in western Wyoming. Its limits, as defined by Executive order of February 22, 1897, are as follows:

Beginning at the southeast corner of township 43 north, range 110 west, sixth principal meridian, Wyoming; thence northerly along the surveyed and unsurveyed range line between ranges 109 and 110 west, to the point of intersection with the south boundary of the Yellowstone National Park Timber Land Reserve, as established by proclamation of September 10, 1891; thence westerly along said boundary to its intersection with the boundary line between the States of Wyoming and Idaho; thence southerly along said State boundary line to the point for the unsurveyed township line between townships 42 and 43 north; thence easterly along the unsurveyed and surveyed township line between townships 42 and 43 north, to the southeast corner of township 43 north, range 110 west, the place of beginning.

In brief, its limits are, on the east, the range line between ranges 109 and 110; on the north, the parallel of 44° north latitude; on the west, the west boundary of Wyoming; and on the south, the south boundary of township 43 north, range 110 west. The area herein included is estimated at 1,300 square miles, or 829,440 acres.

This area has been mapped by the Hayden survey and the United States Geological Survey on a scale of 4 miles to the inch, a scale too small for the representation of details of topography or forest characteristics, but sufficiently large for the presentation of the broader facts of distribution.

The forest conditions of this reserve were examined by Dr. T. S. Brandegee, the well-known botanist of San Diego, Cal. He devoted nearly three months to the examination of this reserve and that portion of the Yellowstone Reserve lying south of Yellowstone Park. This report has been prepared from notes furnished by him.

TOPOGRAPHY.

The principal relief features are simple. Traversing the reserve from north to south, near its western boundary, is the Teton Range, descending rather steeply to the west into the valley of Pierre River, the eastern portion of which is included within the reserve. On the east the mountains descend by a precipitous wall to a broad valley, Jackson Hole, which also traverses the reserve from north to south. East of Jackson Hole the land rises in great, broad mountain spurs to the Wind River Range, whose summit is beyond the limits of the reserve on the east. The area is drained by Snake River and its tributaries southward and westward.

The Teton Range has an average breadth of 12 to 15 miles, and extends northward and southward beyond the limits of the reserve. Its greatest altitude is in the well-known summit, the Grand Teton, which rears its head far above its fellows to an altitude of 13,870 feet. The average altitude of the range probably does not exceed 12,000 feet. The mountains are extremely rugged and rise high above timber line, which is here at an altitude of about 10,000 feet. The only practicable pass in the range is Teton Pass, with an altitude of 8,464 feet. The range has been deeply eroded by glaciers, as well as by water, and there are still in existence several small glaciers occupying little basins high up in the range.

From the crest the range descends on the west quite steeply to the valley known as Teton Basin. The western boundary of the reserve includes a considerable area of this valley, but as the range trends slightly to the westward the strip of valley land diminishes in width southward, so that at the south boundary of the reserve the west line crosses the foothills of the range. The altitude of the valley within the reserve lines ranges from 6,500 to 7,000 feet, an altitude which in this latitude is prohibitive of profitable cultivation except of the hardiest crops, such as potatoes, oats, hay, etc. This valley portion is watered and drained by streams flowing westward to Pierre River from the mountains.

On the east the Teton Range descends by cliffs and slopes of the most rugged character to the valley known as Jackson Hole. This is a broad expanse, extending from the north boundary of the reserve in a direction a little west of south to the southern limit. It has a breadth ranging from 10 to 20 miles, while its altitude within the reserve ranges from 6,500 to 7,000 feet, which, as in the case of Teton Basin, indicates a climate too rigorous for any but the most limited agriculture.

Snake River enters this valley on the north and shortly flows into Jackson Lake, a large body of water 10 miles long by an average of 3 miles in breadth. The river leaves the lake at its southeast angle, and flows at first northeastward, then southeastward, and finally southwestward down the valley, receiving on its way, among other streams,

Buffalo and Gros Ventre rivers from the east and a number of small streams from the west. At the east base of the mountains there is a succession of smaller lakes, among them Lee and Jenny lakes, which are connected and from which flows Lake Creek to the Snake and farther south Taggart and Phelps lakes.

The surface of the valley is, in the main, a gravelly bench land, level and producing a scanty growth of sagebrush, interspersed with a little grass. This bench land terminates with low bluffs, inclosing the bottom lands of the river. These are broad, and through them the river has a very winding course. These bottom lands are covered with a forest of cottonwood and willows, with a dense undergrowth. The river has a great volume at all stages of water, is remarkably uniform in its flow, owing to the existence of a natural reservoir—Jackson Lake—and has a fall amply sufficient to bring the water up to the higher portions of the bench land. Indeed, were it not for the severity of the climate this would form a valuable agricultural region, as there is an abundance of water for irrigation throughout its entire extent.

The northernmost affluent of Snake River from the east is Buffalo River. This stream heads in high, volcanic plateaus east of the reserve, which forms the northward extension of Wind River Range. Its general course is westerly to its junction with the Snake. It is a rapid stream, and flows, through most of its course, in a narrow valley.

North of Buffalo River most of the country is rolling and undulating, not greatly elevated above the level of the river; but it contains numerous isolated fragments of a high plateau about the heads of the streams, many portions of which have been eroded away, and these fragments appear as isolated hills and mesas.

South of Buffalo River, between it and the Gros Ventre, is a high, broad spur stretching westward from the summits to the east. The highest point in this spur is not far from its western end and is known as Mount Leidy, which has an altitude of 11,177 feet. This broad spur or mountain mass is drained mainly southward by the tributaries of Gros Ventre River, the streams flowing to Buffalo River being comparatively short.

Gros Ventre River also heads in the high volcanic plateau and flows with a generally westerly course to its junction with Snake River.

CLIMATE.

So far as I am aware, no observations of rainfall have been made within this area. There is every indication, however, that the rainfall upon the Teton Range and upon the mountain spurs east of Jackson Hole is heavy, especially upon the west slopes of the former range. The existence of glaciers is in itself an indication of a heavy precipitation. The streams flowing from these ranges are large in proportion to their drainage basins, which is another indication of copious rainfall.

In Jackson Hole and Teton Basin, on the other hand, the rainfall is deficient, being inadequate for the needs of agriculture. What little farming is done in these valleys requires irrigation, except in a few localities where the soil is naturally supplied with water by percolation from the streams.

No observations for temperature, so far as I am aware, have been made within this region; but that it is cold—almost subarctic—in temperature may be inferred from the altitude and latitude. The lower portions of the reserve are at an elevation of 6,500 feet, and from that the habitable portions range up to 8,000 feet. The experience of the limited agricultural operations which have been carried on has been sufficient to show, as stated above, that only the hardiest garden vegetables, grains, and forage plants can be cultivated.

AGRICULTURAL LANDS.

As stated above, the west boundary includes a small area in the upper higher part of Teton Basin. This is a triangular tract widest at the north, where it may be 6 miles wide, and diminishing southward to a point. Nearly all of townships 44 and 43 north, range 118 west, are included within this tract. Although elevated and cold, and therefore capable of producing only the hardiest crops, this land is susceptible of irrigation.

Jackson Hole comprises a large amount of agricultural land. It is well situated for irrigation and the supply of water is ample for the entire area. The altitude is, however, great, and the consequent severity of the climate prevents the production of anything but the hardiest vegetables and grains. The value of the land for agriculture, therefore, is not great. The area included in this basin, which may be taken out of the reserve on the ground of its greater value for agriculture than for the production of timber, is as follows:

Range 113 west, township 46 north, three western tiers of sections; township 45 north, south half; range 114 west, townships 46, 45, 44 (north half) north; range 115 west, townships 46, 45, 44, 43 (west half) north; range 116 west, township 44 north, two eastern tiers of sections; township 43 north, east half.

Access to the valley is not easy. From Teton Basin, on the west, a wagon road has been built over Teton Pass, 8,484 feet, over which the mail is carried. This constitutes the principal means of access. From the north end of the valley a trail runs up into Yellowstone Park, and another westward around the north end of Teton Range into Falls River Basin. From the east connection is had with Wind River Valley via Union Pass, at an altitude of 9,516 feet, and Gros Ventre Pass, at an altitude of 9,852 feet, and Buffalo River. From the head of Green River Basin a trail leads to Snake River, at the foot of Jackson Hole, via canyon of Hoback River. The canyon of Snake River at the foot of Jackson Hole is impassable.

GEOLOGY.

The geologic features of this region are very complicated. The entire geologic series is represented, together with a variety of metamorphic rocks and volcanic rocks of all ages.

Teton Range is a monocline, faulted on the east and dipping westward. The body of the range is composed of metamorphic granite. Stratified beds which originally overlaid this have in great part been removed; but upon the summits of certain of the westward spurs patches of Silurian still remain. Lower down Silurian beds lie up against the range continuously from the south end northward for three-fourths the length of the range. Still lower down upon the mountain flank Carboniferous beds overlie Silurian beds, and near the south end of the range Jura Trias beds succeed them. Just above the edge of the valley of Teton River a low, narrow belt of basalt covers the whole breadth of the valley and extends on the north up to the granite upon the range, covering all the stratified beds. At the north end of the range the stratified beds curve around over the granite, showing a succession of Silurian and Carboniferous beds. The central portions of Teton Basin are floored with Quaternary deposits to a great depth.

Jackson Hole occupies the bed of the fault and is, like most of Teton Basin, filled to a great depth with quarternary deposits. In the southern portion are two groups of buttes known, respectively, as Upper and Lower Gros Ventre buttes. The former exposes rocks of Silurian, Carboniferous, and Tertiary ages, while the latter, with a volcanic nucleus, exposes stratified beds of the same ages.

East of Snake River the central geological phenomenon is the elevation of the Gros Ventre range. This is a short range trending northwest and southeast, separating the Gros Ventre and Hoback rivers. It lies, therefore, entirely south of the reserve. This is a short, anticlinal uplift, with a nucleus of granite, and with stratified beds dipping away from it to the northeast, to the southwest, and to the southeast around the end of the range. The succession of the rocks to the northeast shows first a narrow outcrop of Silurian beds, then a broad outcrop of Carboniferous rocks, along the edge of which flows the Gros Ventre River through a part of its course. Succeeding this is an equally broad outcrop of Jura-Trias, whose margin is followed by Gros Ventre River through another part of its course. Succeeding this to the northeast are Cretaceous and Tertiary beds, of which the great mountain spur separating Buffalo River from the Gros Ventre is composed. The other portions of this spur are formed by Tertiary beds.

The country about the head of Gros Ventre and Buffalo rivers is capped by an outflow of volcanic rock lying directly on top of the Tertiary beds, thus protecting them from erosion.

FORESTS.

Although with the exception of Jackson Hole and the other small valley areas above described, and the mountain areas which are above timber line, or are too rugged for timber growth, this region is one in which climatic conditions favor forest growth, yet it contains but little forest. Only a fraction of its area, probably not more than one-fourth, is covered with trees, and most of these are young, small, and of species of little value for lumber. It is only occasionally that tracts of timber of merchantable size are found, and areas containing notable quantities of merchantable forest are few and limited.

This condition appears to be due simply and solely to fires which have swept over the country so completely and persistently that scarcely any part has been entirely exempt from them, while nearly all portions have been burned again and again within a generation. A large proportion of the area has been burned so persistently and frequently that the forests have ceased, temporarily at least, to attempt to restore themselves, and these regions are now grass-covered parks. Indeed, the forest conditions in this reserve closely resemble in all respects those of the Bighorn Mountains. Some areas have been repeatedly burned, so that *Pinus murrayana*, or lodgepole pine, the most abundant conifer, seems to have been driven out. Such areas will naturally become covered with aspen in time, for aspen seeds can be carried great distances by the wind, while lodgepole pine seeds can not spread far from the parent tree except by the aid of birds, squirrels, rats, etc. Under present conditions the tree-bearing regions as a whole decrease, while the aspen areas increase at the expense of those now producing conifers. With few exceptions, young trees are springing up over the recently burned districts, and in most places are abundant. The young growth of lodgepole pine is usually very dense, and even impassable.

The timber of merchantable size and quality is, for the most part, scattered over the reserve in small groves or individual trees, in such wise that except in a few localities it could not be cut economically. These few localities are specified in the detailed descriptions which follow. Altogether they are estimated to contain 22,180 acres, or about the equivalent of a township. Thus, only about 3 per cent of the area of the reserve is covered by merchantable timber in anything like compact bodies. These areas are estimated to contain about 75,000,000 feet B. M.

The entire area of the reserve is approximately 1,300 square miles. Of this, 300 square miles are without timber, because of great altitude or the rugged character of the country, 250 square miles of this being rugged portions of the Teton Range, and the remainder is comprised in the elevated summits of the volcanic plateau on the eastern border of the reserve. In the Teton Basin there is an area of about 25 square miles within the reserve, which is naturally timberless, and in Jackson Hole there is a similar area of 150 square miles. These two areas probably never will produce timber because of deficient rainfall.

In addition to these are the areas of Jackson and other lakes, estimated to comprise 41 square miles. There is thus altogether an area of 515 square miles, or 40 per cent of the entire area of the reserve, which is not only without timber at present, but is, in all probability, incapable of supporting a timber growth. Of the remaining 785 square miles, all of which is believed to be capable of producing timber, only 38 per cent at present has a growth of timber upon it, and only 3.5 per cent of the latter area contains timber of merchantable size and quantity. These areas of merchantable timber, which, as stated above, comprise in all the equivalent of about one township, contain an estimated amount of 75,000,000 feet B. M. of timber. If the entire area of 875 square miles were timbered as heavily as are these few areas, the reserve would contain about 1,000,000,000 feet instead of 75,000,000. The difference between these two figures represents the destruction by fire.

SPECIES OF TIMBER.

The timber trees found on this reserve are: *Pinus murrayana*, which forms the bulk of the forest; Aspens, next in abundance, and *Picea engelmanni*, *Abies subalpina*, *Pinus flexilis*, and finally the cottonwoods. Their relative abundance and distribution are shown below.

Pinus murrayana (*Lodgepole pine*).—This comprises four-fifths of the coniferæ. It is here a small tree, rarely 2 feet in diameter and 75 feet high. When growing alone a tree commonly bears limbs low down upon the trunk, but in a forest, and growing close together, it may have a clear trunk for 30 feet. It covers large areas to the exclusion of all other trees, and then its trunk is rarely more than 8 to 12 inches in diameter, although 50 to 75 feet high. It grows from the lowest elevation to 8,000 or even 9,000 feet, but is more plentiful at the lowest and middle elevations. The dead dry logs of these trees furnish material for the log houses and fences of the inhabitants. The larger ones are culled out by the sawmills and known as "bird's-eye" pine. The boards made from it are white and full of knots.

Picea engelmanni (*Engelmann spruce*).—The habitat of this tree is along streams between elevations of 7,000 to 10,000 feet. It is in some places abundant, and seems to furnish most of the logs for the sawmills.

A large tree may be 3 feet in diameter and 125 feet high. Its habitat and situation on damp soil often prevent its destruction by fire.

Pseudotsuga taxifolia (red fir).—This is nowhere very abundant. It grows usually on dry ridges, and since much of it survives the fires it is probably relatively more abundant than if the rest of the forest had not been destroyed. It is especially prominent on the west side of the Teton Range, above Lee Creek. The largest trees are 3 feet in diameter and more than 100 feet high. It is not sufficiently abundant to be of any value as a timber tree.

Populus tremuloides.—The aspen, after *P. murrayana*, is the most common tree. It grows from the lowest elevation to 8,000 or 9,000 feet. It is commonly small, rarely growing 2 feet in diameter and 50 feet high. It is especially abundant at the lower elevations along the edge of the coniferæ.

Populus augustifolia (aspen).—This tree grows only along the streams in the valleys. It is abundant along Snake River, Spread Creek, and Pacific Creek, and is found also on the streams west of the Teton Range. The trees grow to 3 or 4 feet in diameter and 75 feet high. These cottonwoods are used for fencing on the west side, where it is difficult to get *P. murrayana*. Following the streams, it extends farther than the coniferæ into the agricultural areas.

Populus trichocarpa (cottonwood).—This is not common. It is usually found with *P. augustifolia*. A few trees grow along Spread Creek, more about Jenny and Taggart lakes and on the western side of the Teton Range.

Juniperus communis (juniper).—This juniper is very uncommon; only a bush seen now and then, perhaps two dozen altogether.

Juniperus virginiana (red juniper).—Very little of this tree is found. About Miners Ferry some posts of it have been used.

Pinus flexilis.—This species grows in exposed situations and rarely covers any area. There are some good-sized forests south from Togwotee Pass. It is usually common near the timber-line region, along the summit of ridges, and sometimes a solitary tree grows out on the plains. It is not used for lumber because of its inaccessible habitat and its short trunk.

Abies subalpina.—This is most abundant about the timber line on northern slopes, and sometimes follows the streams down to the lowest elevations. The largest trees are 2 or 3 feet in diameter and 100 feet high, but it is considered worthless for lumber. The bark is thin, and the tree is thus easily killed by fire, but as it generally grows in moist situations much escapes burning.

UNDERGROWTH.

Pinus murrayana woods never have a very heavy undergrowth, and it is often entirely wanting. There is little humus in these forests. The most abundant vegetation growing under *P. murrayana* is "pine grass," a grass not relished by stock. In moist situations lonicera is common, with ribes, shepherdia, etc. Two or three species of shrubby artemisia are very abundant in almost every place where there is no forest; but in the forest there is usually very little undergrowth of shrubs. The most abundant is vaccinium of two or three species in the subalpine and middle elevations. Eleagnus is abundant along the stream banks of the lower elevations. Among the herbaceous plants that are valuable for pasturage or for hay, and are abundant, geranium, balsamorrhiga, and helianthella are the most important.

Ceanothus velutinus is common east of Jackson Lake, north of Pacific Creek, on the east slope of the Teton Range, and west of the range. This bush is at times conspicuous on areas burned several years previous. *Sphaeralcea acerifolia*, a showy malvaceous shrub, soon appears in a burned district with epilobium, etc.

DETAILED DESCRIPTION.

The reserve includes townships 43 to 46, inclusive, in ranges 110 to 118, inclusive; in all, 36 entire or fractional townships. In only a small part of the reserve have the township lines been run. The following description applies, in the main, to townships as hereafter to be laid out:

Township 46 north, range 110 west.—This township lies close to the high mountain divide separating the waters of Wind River from those of the Snake. It is composed of high, rugged, plateau-like mountain spurs, between which are the heads of streams flowing to Buffalo River. The altitude ranges from 8,000 to 11,000 feet. There is very little timber, and that is on the lower slopes of the valleys of the streams, the summits of the ridges and plateau being bare.

Township 46 north, range 111 west.—The eastern part of this township is made up of spurs from the Snake-Wind River Divide, between which flow in high valleys branches of Buffalo River. The western portion is comparatively low, undulating country, in which is the valley of the North Fork of Buffalo River. The altitude ranges from 7,500 feet up to 10,000. The timber is scattering. The undulating country of the western portion is covered by groves alternating with parks. Upon the lower slopes of the high mountain ridges there is scattering timber. The ridge rising in the southeastern portion of the township is well covered with forests.

Township 46 north, range 112 west.—The country is high and rolling, with an average altitude of about 8,000 feet, and is drained by the waters of Pacific Creek and those of Buffalo River. The slopes to Pacific Creek in the northern part of the township are fairly well timbered, while upon the drainage to Buffalo River, which occupies the southern two-thirds of the township, timber is scattering, occurring only in groves upon the north slopes, and contains much dead timber. There are two small recent burns in the north edge of the township.

Township 46 north, range 113 west.—Pacific Creek flows southwest across this township and drains the entire area. The surface presents no great relief, excepting a high, abrupt hill on the eastern edge and quite high bluffs along the creek. The altitude ranges from 7,000 to 9,000 feet. A large part of this township, perhaps one-third of it, has recently been burned. This burned area is east of Pacific Creek. The slopes on the south side of the creek are fairly well timbered, and timber occurs in patches elsewhere. In the southwestern part of the township there is much quaking aspen and cottonwood, mingled with young pines, in the valley of the creek. The northwestern part of the township contains scattered groves of young conifers, with much dead timber standing or fallen.

Township 46 north, range 114 west.—This township also is made up of rolling and broken country, disposed rather irregularly, and is in the main drained by a small creek flowing directly into Jackson Lake. Most of its area is devoid of timber. Some quaking aspen groves are found in the southern part and along the creek, while in the northwestern part are areas of small conifers. Three small recent burns have occurred in the northwestern portion of the township.

Township 46 north, range 115 west.—This township contains the northern portion of Jackson Lake. The country generally is level, having an elevation of approximately 7,000 feet. Snake River enters the northwestern portion of the township and flows southward into the head of the lake. On its eastern bank is a strip of open valley country, perhaps a mile in width and 2 miles in length north and south. This is a fine meadow, from which many tons of hay were cut in 1877 and many more might have been cut. The soil is damp from seepage from the river, so that no irrigation is needed for the production of hay. On the west bank the river is bordered by a belt of cottonwoods. East of the lake is a mixture of pines and aspens, mainly the former, which in the northeastern part of the township becomes somewhat dense, but is entirely composed of young trees. Among them are two or three small recent burns. On the west shore of the lake is a fairly heavy growth of pines, extending from the shore back to the foot of the mountains and running up into the gulches in places for a mile or two. This area, which extends westward into range 116, contains a body of merchantable timber of more than 2,000 feet to the acre, over an area of nearly seven sections.

Township 46 north, range 116 west.—Nearly all of this township is occupied by the high, rugged Teton Range, and is entirely devoid of timber, owing to the combined effects of altitude and ruggedness. Along its eastern edge, however, the belt of timber fringing Jackson Lake extends over into this township for a mile or two near the northern line.

Township 46 north, range 117 west.—This township is occupied by the Teton Range. With the exception of the northwestern quarter, it is barren. There is a strip of timber upon the western edge consisting of young pines, with some red fir and scattered aspens. This area of timber, which extends into the next township westward and southwestward is one of the largest in the reserve.

Township 46 north, range 118 west.—This township contains the west slope of the Teton Range. It consists of long spurs and narrow valleys running westward. The body of timber covering this township, the western portion of township 46, range 117, and the northern portion of township 45, range 118, is composed mainly of young lodgepole pines of various ages and sizes from 10 feet high upward. Its distribution depends upon the topography. Innumerable small gulches and depressions run from the mountains westward. On their northern slopes and in the bottoms there is an impassable second growth of pine, with more or less fallen dead timber. Young aspens grow about the edges and on the northern slopes. On these slopes, also, there are often large red firs. These trees, however, are in many other places very large in proportion to other trees of the locality, because they are not killed easily by fire, and may therefore have survived several generations of aspens and *Pinus murrayana*. In some localities in this area patches of good-sized *Pinus murrayana* and also aspens are seen, but the trees of this species are mainly young and so dense that the region is impassable in a north and south direction. A part of this area, comprising nearly eleven sections, is estimated to contain over 2,000 feet of standing timber to the acre of merchantable size and quality.

Township 45 north, range 110 west.—This township presents high relief, being composed of the deep valleys of the head branches of Buffalo River, between which are high plateau-like spurs. The sides of these spurs are partially covered with forests, while the summits and upper portions of the slopes are bare.

Township 45 north, range 111 west.—This township is traversed from east to west by the narrow valley of Buffalo River, and from its north boundary nearly to its south boundary by the valley of the North Fork of that river. The southern part of the township is composed of a mountain spur, separating Buffalo from Black Rock Creek, while north of Buffalo River on the east of its North Fork is another high spur. These spurs reach altitudes of 11,000 feet, and, as the valley of Buffalo River is 7,400 feet, the range of altitude in this township exceeds 3,500 feet. North of Buffalo River and west of its North Fork the country is undulating, with but slight relief.

The spur south of Buffalo River is fairly well timbered upon its north face, in small areas across its summit, and down the southern face. This timber is of commercial size and will cut over 2,000 feet per acre over an area equivalent to two sections. In the western part of the township upon this spur is a burn, covering some four or five square miles. Much of the dead timber is still standing and is mainly Engelmann's fir. This is among the largest of this species seen upon the reserve, and if not burned would have been among the largest seen upon the reserve, many trees being 2 feet in diameter and 100 feet high. If not killed by fire this would have been one of the most valuable bodies of timber seen.

On the southern slope of the spur north of Buffalo River and east of its North Fork there is quite a body of timber, covering perhaps three-fourths of the surface. Around on the west end of this spur the timber becomes much more scattering, only a small fraction of the surface being covered by it. On the north slopes again the timber becomes close, while the top of the spur is entirely bare. West of the North Fork the undulating country contains only scattered groves of timber.

Township 45 north, range 112 west.—This township is traversed by Buffalo River from east to west in a valley from 1 to 2 miles in width. South of it this valley is separated from that of Black Rock Creek by a low, flat ridge rising 600 or 800 feet above the valley. Near the center of the township Box Creek enters Buffalo River. On the north and east of this creek the country is undulating, presenting a slight relief. West of it is a high symmetrical hill lying partly in this township and partly in township 45 north, range 113 west, whose summit is about 2,500 feet above the valley, or 9,500 feet above the sea.

The immediate valley of Buffalo River is treeless. The low, flat ridge separating it from Black Rock Creek is in part covered by scattering groves and in part by a burn of some 4 or 5 square miles. Within this township, as noted in describing township 45 north, range 111 west, this burn is covered with standing and fallen *Pinus engelmanni* of merchantable size. North of Buffalo River and east of Black Rock Creek the undulating country is covered by scattered groves, mainly of young trees. The hill lying west of this creek is covered by a scattering growth of aspens, young pines, and a few red firs, with a large amount of standing and fallen dead timber.

Township 45 north, range 113 west.—This township is traversed from east to west by Buffalo River, which crosses it near its southern border in a valley from 1 to 2 miles in width. Were it not for the elevation, this valley would be valuable agricultural land. On the east line of the township Black Rock Creek enters Buffalo River, and near the junction is located one of the few ranches in the reserve. The soil of the valley is largely coarse gravel, in which the river has cut many courses. On the south of the valley there is a low bluff on which are scattered groves of aspen, and on the north the country rises into hills. On the east side of the township the country rises to a height of 9,500 feet above the sea. The slopes are covered with aspen groves and a scattered growth of young pines, with a few old red firs. Among this young growth many dead pines are still standing, while the ground is covered with others which have fallen. Upon the western side of the township is a second hill, rising about 2,500 feet above the valley. On this there are a few scattered groves of pine, but most of the slopes of this hill, with the flat country north of it, have been recently burned. The summit is entirely devoid of timber.

Township 45 north, range 114 west.—In the western portion of this township is the outlet of Jackson Lake. Snake River flows at first eastward with a very crooked course to the junction of Pacific Creek, where it turns southward. The township also contains the lower courses of Pacific Creek and Buffalo River. The surface presents very little relief. It is mostly low, rising but slightly above the level of the lake, the shores of which, as well as the banks of Snake River just below the lake, are marshy. Most of the northwestern part of the township in the neighborhood of the lake is covered with willows. An agricultural area extends into the next township west and has a fine deep soil, free from gravel. If cleared of brush it would become a fine hay meadow. There are at present two ranches upon it. The remaining country west of Pacific Creek is largely open, with a few scattering groves of pine and aspen. Between the mouths of Pacific Creek and Buffalo River on the lower hill slopes are also groves of aspen and pine, and on the slopes of the ridge south of Buffalo River are also groves of aspen.

Township 45 north, range 115 west.—This township contains the southern portion of Jackson Lake. The land is level and raised but little above the lake. The northeastern portion of the east shore of Jackson Lake is covered with scattered groves of pine and aspen and farther eastward with willows and grass. The eastern shores of the lake, comprised in the southern part of the township, are covered with a scattered growth of young pines. This region has been so frequently burned, down to the present time, that in the eastern part the pine seems to have difficulty in reproducing itself. In the western part, however, it is coming up very densely, so that, with the thickets of young pines and the network of fallen dead timber, the region is almost impassable. Here also many red firs are found, which appear to have survived a succession of fires. In the northwest, at the base of Teton Range, is a small area of heavy timber.

Township 45 north, range 116 west.—This township is comprised almost entirely in the Teton Range. In the eastern part there is included a portion of the west shores of Jackson Lake, which are timbered up to the foot of the steep mountains.

Township 45 north, range 117 west.—This township is entirely comprised in the Teton Range and contains almost no timber, except near the western borders, where a scattering growth begins to come in.

Township 45 north, range 118 west.—This township is situated at the west foot of the Teton Range, where the steep slopes flatten down into Teton Basin, and contains the southern portion of the largest continuous body of timber in the reserve. The timber is young lodge-pole pine, with more or less fallen dead timber, and here and there scattered through the young forests are old red firs. In the southern part of this township the timber becomes much more scattering, and the pines are largely replaced by groves of aspen. A small, narrow burn traverses this township up the north slopes of the spur to the region north of Lee Creek.

Township 44 north, range 110 west.—The northeastern half of this township consists of an elevated plateau, about 11,000 feet above the sea, considerably above the limit of timber. This elevated table-land descends by a cliff 1,000 or more feet in height to a valley running northwest and southeast, in which heads Black Rock Creek on one side and a stream flowing to Wind River on the other. The summit in the valley between these two streams is Togwotee Pass, which has an elevation of 9,400 feet. Most of this valley, which is between 1 and 2 miles in width, is well timbered. The southwestern portion of the township is occupied by a group of hills rising to an altitude of about 11,000 feet. The slopes of these hills, up to an altitude of 10,000 feet, are also well timbered with pine of merchantable size, bearing over 2,000 feet to the acre, over an area of 2¼ sections.

Township 44 north, range 111 west.—The northeastern part of this township is crossed by Black Rock Creek in a broad valley nearly 2 miles in width. On the northeast are the slopes of the high plateau noted in the description of township 44 north, range 110 west, which are here covered with a light scattering growth of conifers. The valley itself is a succession of high mountain meadows with no trees except willows. On the southeast the land rises into irregular hills, which separate the waters of Black Rock Creek from those of Gros Ventre River. These support scattering groves of conifers, which are estimated to cover from one-half to two-thirds of the surface of the western part of the township, with a number of small burns, which altogether aggregate a number of square miles.

Township 44 north, range 112 west.—This township is crossed from east to west by Elkhorn Creek, on either side of which rise broken, irregular hills, separating it on the north from the waters of Black Rock Creek and on the south from those of Gros Ventre River. The township is covered with groves of conifers interspersed with open areas, the timber covering from one-half to two-thirds of the surface. The trees are all young, and among them is much dead standing timber, while the ground is thickly covered with fallen trees. There are two burns of considerable importance—one about 3 miles in length by 1 mile in width, lying along the north bank of Elkhorn Creek, and the other south of that stream, comprising, perhaps, 2 square miles.

Township 44 north, range 113 west.—The south line of this township passes over the summit of Mount Leidy. From the group of hills, of which this is the principal summit, the land falls northward to the canyon of Elkhorn Creek, then rises again in low hills, separating the latter from the waters of Buffalo River. The Mount Leidy group of hills is timbered with conifers up to an altitude of about 10,000 feet. These are quite heavy on the north slopes, averaging over 2,000 feet per acre over an area equivalent to four sections in this and the adjoining township on the west. North of Elkhorn Creek the high portion of the hills contains groves of conifers, covering, perhaps, one-half of the surface, while at the lower altitudes the timber changes into aspen groves.

Township 44 north, range 114 west.—The southern portion of this township consists of the north slopes of high hills separating the Snake from Gros Ventre rivers, and descending to the valley of the former stream. These northern slopes are covered quite densely by young lodge-pole pines 15 to 20 feet in height, while in the southeast the trees reach merchantable size. The lower ground at the base of these slopes contains scattered groves of aspen, while the northern portion of the township includes the immediate valley and bottom lands of Snake River, and is open, with the exception of a belt immediately along Snake River covered with cottonwoods and willows.

Township 44 north, range 115 west.—This township is practically comprised in the valley of Jackson Hole. It is crossed by Snake River flowing southwest in a broad bottom land which is timbered with cottonwoods and willows over an area perhaps a mile in width. On the northwest is a broad bench of gravelly soil covered with sagebrush. On the northern edge is a small body of young pines interspersed with areas of recent burns.

Township 44 north, range 116 west.—The eastern third of this township is comprised of the level expanse of Jackson Hole and includes Jenny Lake and part of Leigh Lake, which are glacial lakes, lying at the immediate foot of the Teton Range. The western two-thirds of the township are composed of high and rugged spurs of the range. The Grand Teton, the crowning summit, is in the southwest corner of the township. The eastern edge of the township is open and covered with a sparse growth of sage. The shores of Jenny Lake are timbered, the timber extending in a scattering way up the spurs and the gorge of a creek flowing into the lake. The most of the timber on Leigh Lake has been burned. The mountainous portion of the township is almost entirely devoid of timber, being too rugged and too high for a forest growth.

Township 44 north, range 117 west.—This township is entirely comprised in the Teton Range, and contains very little timber. This little is in the form of groves of pine scattered over the lower portions of the west half of the township.

Township 44 north, range 118 west.—This township comprises the lower slopes of the Teton Range and extends into Teton Basin. The east half contains a little pine timber, mainly in scattering groves, but in the canyons of Lee and Teton creeks, especially on the south side of the latter, are small bodies of good timber, averaging over 5,000 feet to the acre. In each of these canyons there is a sawmill established, which is engaged in utilizing the timber. The western half of the township, which is comparatively level, is covered in the upper part by aspen groves and in the lower part is open and covered with grass. This area of open country, which extends south over the western half of township 43, range 118, is all good agricultural land and all "claimed" by persons most of whom live upon their ranches. Some ranches have fine berry gardens. The land is all easily irrigable from the mountain streams. The main crops are potatoes and turnips. Oats and barley can also be raised. The money-making industry, however, is cattle raising, with the production of butter, etc. The soil is fine, deep, and free from gravel. The nearer the foothills the finer and better the soil.

Township 43 north, range 110 west.—This township comprises high hills or mountains rising to an altitude of 10,000 feet at the heads of branches of Wind River and the Gros Ventre. One-third to one-half is timbered with groves of conifers, alternating with open parks.

Township 43 north, range 111 west.—This township is made up of southward slopes from the divide between Black Rock Creek and Gros Ventre River and the valley of a tributary to the latter stream. The slopes are sparsely timbered with groves of conifers. The valley of the tributary is open, while immediately south of it, in the southern part of the township, the country is covered with aspen groves.

Township 43 north, range 112 west.—Across this township, from west to east, flows a branch of Gros Ventre River, while north and south of it hills rise to altitudes of nearly 10,000 feet. The township is sparsely timbered, perhaps one-third of the area being covered with groves of conifers interspersed with much dead timber. The living trees are young and small and there are numerous small burns, especially in the western part of the township.

Township 43 north, range 113 west.—This township is drained southward by Gros Ventre River, which flows in a broad, open, timberless valley. Southeast of its valley are low hills with a few groves of conifers, while the northwest two-thirds of the township are composed or hills rising westward to altitudes of 9,500 feet and northward to the summit of Mount Leidy, on the north township line. These hills are sparsely covered with groves of conifers, about one-fourth of the area being wooded and the remainder parks.

Township 43 north, range 114 west.—This township is made up of the southward slope of the hills which separate Buffalo from Gros Ventre rivers. It is sparsely covered with scattered groves of conifers, covering perhaps one-fourth of the area, the remainder being open parks.

Township 43 north, range 115 west.—The eastern part of this township is hilly, being the eastern slopes of the spur separating Buffalo and Snake rivers from the Gros Ventre. These spurs are sparsely covered with groves of aspen and a few conifers on the lower parts. The remainder of the township consists of the open valley of Jackson Hole. The Snake River flows across the northwest part of the township in a broad bottom land timbered with cottonwoods and willows. Upper Gros Ventre Butte rises from the middle of the valley upon the southwest corner of the township. This butte, rising to an altitude of 1,000 feet above the valley, is pretty well timbered at the northern end, while the greater part is covered with scattered groves of conifers. The valley is floored with good soil, 3 to 5 feet deep, mostly free from gravel, and easily irrigated from Dutch Creek. All the water was taken from this creek this year by settlers.

Township 43 north, range 116 west.—The eastern two-thirds of this township lies in Jackson Hole. It is level, and across the southeast corner flows Snake River in a broad bottom land covered with cottonwoods and willows. Back of this, on each side, is a belt of gravelly land covered with a sparse growth of sage. Succeeding this on the west is a broad belt 2 miles in width of fairly good timber. Some of this, over an area estimated at 2 square miles, contains over 2,000 feet per acre. The western third of the township comprises the cliffs of the eastern descent of the Teton Range. It contains very little timber, and that of scrubby character, consisting of the few conifers that find a footing among the rocks.

Township 43 north, range 117 west.—This township is entirely comprised in one of the most rugged portions of the Teton Range. It is without timber, except in the few scattering trees in the southeast corner and a small body in the canyon of Darby Creek, in the southwest corner.

Township 43 north, range 118 west.—This township comprises the lower slopes of the Teton Range and the eastern border of Teton Basin. Most of the area is timbered, but upon the canyon walls of the creeks are scattered groves of conifers, and upon Darby Creek, in the southern part of the township, is a small but valuable body of timber, averaging over 5,000 feet per acre, for the utilization of which a sawmill has been established near the foot of the canyon. The western portion of the township is level, open, and covered with sage.

With this tier of townships the reservation, as established by the order of President Cleveland of February 27, 1897, ends. Examination was made, however, of the three tiers of townships lying farther south, and the description will be extended to include these townships.

Township 42 north, range 110 west.—This township is composed of high hills on the northeast side of Gros Ventre River, the summits of which have altitudes exceeding 10,000 feet. The eastern half of the township is from one-half to three-fourths covered with coniferous timber and the west half with scattered groves of aspens, covering perhaps one-third of its surface.

Township 42 north, range 111 west.—This township is crossed from southeast to northwest by Gros Ventre River, flowing in a narrow valley, while in the northwestern part it is crossed by a creek which enters the Gros Ventre near the western boundary of the township. South of the Gros Ventre the hills which border its valley are covered with small groves of conifers, changing into aspen in the valley. North of the river the hills are covered with scattered groves of conifers, changing into aspen in the northern and eastern portion of the township.

Township 42 north, range 112 west.—This township is crossed by Gros Ventre River flowing first southwest and then northwest. Its valley is from 1 to 2 miles in width and is covered with cottonwoods and willows. South of the river there is very little timber except in the southwest corner, which contains scattered groves of conifers. On the northern side the land rises gradually and is almost barren of timber, the lower slopes containing a little aspen, while higher up are scattered groves of coniferous trees.

Township 42 north, range 113 west.—This township is crossed by Gros Ventre River in a broad and almost barren valley. The hills to the north are entirely treeless, with the exception of an area of 1 or 2 square miles in the northwest corner of the township. South of the river the land rises gradually into hills, the lower slopes of which are almost treeless, but higher up there is a dense growth of coniferous trees, which, over an area of 2 sections in this township, average 2,000 feet or more per acre. The summit of the hills is treeless.

Township 42 north, range 114 west.—This township also is crossed by Gros Ventre River, flowing a little north of east in a rather narrow valley. North of the stream there is practically no timber. South the hills rise abruptly to a high summit of 11,000 feet. These slopes are very well timbered; over an area of 4 sections it is estimated that the timber exceeds 2,000 feet per acre, although some of this has been recently burned.

Township 42 north, range 115 west.—This is crossed by the Gros Ventre, flowing somewhat south of west in a valley which at first is narrow and then opens out into Jackson Hole. The southeastern part of this township is mountainous, forming the western end of the spur separating Gros Ventre River from little Gros Ventre Creek. The higher portions of these hills and their northern slopes contain some conifers. On the lower slopes are groves of aspen. The level portions of the township, those within Jackson Hole, are mainly covered with sage and grass.

Township 42 north, range 116 west.—This township is comprised entirely in the valley of Jackson Hole. On the south line of this township the Gros Ventre joins the Snake. The surface of the township is level, except for river benches. The rivers are bordered by broad belts of cottonwood and willows. The bench lines are in the main covered with sage and grass. Few conifers are found in the northwest corner of the township.

Township 42 north, range 117 west.—This township is mostly comprised in the Teton Range, the southeast corner only being within Jackson Hole. This portion is covered with sage and grass, and the streams coming down from the mountains have formed sloughs and meadows, from which considerable hay is cut. The mountains are almost entirely treeless, with the exception of a few small groves of conifers on the lower slopes.

Township 42 north, range 118 west.—This township is almost entirely comprised in the Teton Range and contains very little timber except in the canyons of Darby and Fox creeks. The former stream, especially, has a fairly good body of timber on it. Aside from these two canyons the only timber is found in a few groves scattered over the lower slopes.

Township 41 north, range 110 west.—This township is traversed by the upper waters of Gros Ventre River, flowing northeastward across it in a narrow valley. The hills on each side are fairly well covered with conifers.

Township 41 north, range 111 west.—This township is traversed by branches of Gros Ventre River, between which is a high, rolling country. It contains very little timber; large areas have been recently burned.

Township 41 north, range 112 west.—This township is drained by a creek flowing north across it into Gros Ventre River. The land rises gently from the valley of this creek on the eastward, and is almost treeless. West of this creek are scattered groves of conifers, covering perhaps one-half the area.

Township 41 north, range 113 west.—This township is traversed from south to north by a branch of Gros Ventre River. From its valley the land rises steeply to high, plateau-like summits, with an altitude of 10,000 to 11,000 feet. The township contains very little timber, neither the slopes nor the summits of these plateaus being forested.

Township 41 north, range 114 west.—This township is drained by Little Gros Ventre Creek. From its narrow, canyon-like valley the land rises steeply several thousand feet to the summit of high plateaus, between 10,000 and 11,000 feet in altitude. The canyon walls of this stream are fairly well timbered. Elsewhere timber occurs only in small groves and bunches, while the summit of the plateau is everywhere bare.

Township 41 north, range 115 west.—This township is made up in the main of extremely broken country, draining into Gros Ventre River. On Pollock Creek, one of the branches, is a considerable body of good timber. Elsewhere timber occurs only in patches of small area, and consists entirely of conifers.

Township 41 north, range 116 west.—This township lies in the main within Jackson Hole, and contains the lower Gros Ventre buttes and the western end of the mountain mass lying south of Little Gros Ventre Creek. Besides a few scattered groves of conifers, the township contains no timber, except on the western end of the upper Gros Ventre buttes, lying in the northwest corner of the township. This is well timbered with conifers.

Township 41 north, range 117 west.—At least half of this township lies within Jackson Hole, and is traversed by Snake River from north to south and by Fighting Bear Creek. That part of the level valley lying between the river and Fighting Bear Creek contains scattered groves of lodge-pole pine and Engelmann fir, with open parks and a little cottonwood. The western part of the township is in the Teton

Range, and contains several patches of timber of some importance. One of these, 3 or 4 miles square, lies on the mountain spur. Another is on the south wall of East Pass Creek, where there is a sawmill engaged in cutting lumber for local consumption.

Township 41 north, range 118 west.—This township is comprised within the range, and its surface is extremely rugged. On the south canyon wall of Trail Creek, which flows westward from the pass, is a considerable body of good timber, and there are a few small patches scattered about elsewhere on the mountain spurs.

Township 40 north, range 110 west.—This township comprises high, rolling country about the heads of Gros Ventre River. This area is perhaps two-thirds covered by young pines.

Township 40 north, range 111 west.—The surface of the country is entirely similar to that of the township last described, being high and rolling, but there is scarcely any timber on it.

Township 40 north, range 112 west.—This township also lies high, being at the heads of branches of Gros Ventre River, and consists of a rather undulating country. It is estimated that half its area is covered with groves of pine.

Township 40 north, range 113 west.—This township is intersected by the gorges of streams flowing into Gros Ventre River. The country is high and broken and contains no timber.

Township 40 north, range 114 west.—This township is very similar to the one last described, being high, broken, and timberless.

Township 40 north, range 115 west.—This township comprises the summit of the hills from which flow the waters of Little Gros Ventre Creek. It is high and broken, and the only timber contained on it is in a few scattered groves.

Township 40 north, range 116 west.—The eastern part of this township comprises the lower slopes of the hills in which Little Gros Ventre River collects its waters. These hills are almost timberless, the forest consisting of scattered groves of trees. The western half is in the valley of Jackson Hole. It is a level country covered with sage and brush.

Township 40 north, range 117 west.—The northeastern portion of this township is in Jackson Hole, the level portion being sharply outlined by Snake River, which flows southeast across the corner of the township, closely hugging the foot of the Teton Mountains. The western part of the township, including fully three-fourths of it, is included within the range, the northeast slopes of which are fairly well timbered.

Township 40 north, range 118 west.—This township is entirely comprised of the Teton range, and owing to its high and rugged character contains no timber whatever.

SAWMILLS.

The sawmills operating in this reserve and its vicinity are few and of small capacity. One that is off the reserve is situated east of the Teton Pass, and is now (1877) in operation. The market must mainly consist of the settlers of Jackson Hole, for the steep road over the pass will prevent any heavy load being hauled over it.

Darby Creek sawmill.—This is a new mill which has just gone into operation. In addition to a sawmill, there is also a mill for "finishing" lumber. To this mill the inhabitants of Teton Basin look for lumber. There is said to be 1,000,000 feet above it, and the estimate does not appear excessive. All the mills saw mainly *P. engelmanni*, but also cull out the large *P. murrayana*, and a red fir if near is, of course, also cut. The logs are 20 to 30 feet long, but the lumber has many knots. The logs for this mill will be cut from the low, damp ground above.

No sawmills are on the Yellowstone Reserve, but some lumber was sawed by a Government contractor for the soldiers' quarters and the bridge over the Snake. The trees to be sawed were "culled out." The mill was a portable one.

Teton Creek sawmill.—This is an old mill, having been in operation, it is said, nine years. The mill is supposed to be nearly worn out and it seems certain that there is no more timber of any account to be sawed. It is sawing now on an "order." The quantity of timber sawed is not known, but is probably not a large amount, as little is required to supply the needs of a community that builds log houses and pole fences.

Lee Creek sawmill.—This mill has not cut very much, and has been ordered out by the Government. It has permission to saw the logs on hand, about seventy-five, and have piles of lumber made from about the same number. There does not seem to be so much lumber to be cut as above the Darby Creek mill. All the mills saw mainly *P. engelmanni*. It is the largest tree with the largest trunk.

ROADS AND TRAILS.

It seems hardly necessary to discuss fully the practicability of transporting lumber in a country that has so little that is merchantable. The distance from a market is so great and the timber is so poor that it will probably never be exported, even if a railway should be built through the valley. There will, however, be a small home demand. There is a road of easy grades up the Snake to the Yellowstone Park which would also be good to Victor and Teton Basin but for the exceedingly steep grades about Teton Pass. The road from the United States military station by Grassy Lakes to Fall River has very easy grades so far as I have seen it, and is said to be excellent its whole length. Logs could be easily floated down Buffalo Creek and Gros Ventre, both large streams, and roads can easily be constructed up their valleys well into the mountains.

GAME.

Great numbers of elk come down from Yellowstone Park and feed in the high mountains during the summer. In the winter, when they are driven by cold and deep snows to seek their food at lower elevations, their number is much increased. The settlements of the Teton Basin and regions west of the mountains have very much restricted their winter feeding grounds, and the settlement of Jackson Hole increases the difficulty of finding winter feed. It is said that a thousand died from starvation in Jackson Hole last winter.

RANCHES.

There were within the reserve, at the time of its examination, about 40 ranches, 19 of which were on the eastern edge of the Teton Basin and 21 in Jackson Hole. These are, in the main, small cattle ranches, on which there is practically no cultivation of the soil. The cattle range during the summer and wild hay is cut for their winter subsistence. Jackson Hole and the neighboring mountains being a resort for fishermen and sportsmen, much of the business of the settlers in this valley consists in supplying these tourists with outfits and supplies.

Owing to the hostility of the present residents of Jackson Hole and the Teton Basin, all of whom are cattlemen, there are no sheep within the reserve. The number of cattle and horses in Jackson Hole is very small, being limited by the amount of forage which can be cut and stored for winter use. At present they range in the valley, to all parts of which their range does not yet extend.

YELLOWSTONE PARK RESERVE, SOUTHERN PART.

Limits and topography.—This reserve lies east and south of Yellowstone Park. The portion south of the park, lying between its south boundary and the north boundary of the Teton Reserve, which is the parallel of 44° north latitude, and between the one hundred and tenth meridian and the west boundary of Wyoming, was examined by Dr. T. S. Brandegee, and the following report has been prepared from notes furnished by him:

This portion of the Yellowstone Park Reserve has a breadth from north to south of approximately 10 miles, and its length east and west is 51 miles. It comprises an area of 510 square miles, or 326,400 acres. The eastern part is drained northward by Upper Yellowstone River, while the greater portion of it is drained southward by Snake River and its tributaries.

The elevation of the region is great, ranging from 7,000 to over 10,000 feet, with an average elevation probably between 8,000 and 9,000 feet.

Upper Yellowstone River enters near the southeast corner and flows northwestward across the reserve in a marshy valley about a mile in width. East of the river the land rises to a high plateau 9,000 to 10,000 feet in altitude. West of it the country between the river and Atlantic Creek, which heads in Two Ocean Pass, is plateau-like in character, with summits exceeding 10,000 feet in altitude, and is much dissected by streams. The Continental Divide, separating the Upper Yellowstone from the drainage of Snake River, has a general altitude of about 10,000 feet, but is broken by several passes at much lower altitudes. The well-known Two Ocean Pass, in which head Atlantic and Pacific creeks, which have water communication, has an elevation of 8,200 feet. A pass separating Mink and Falcon creeks is slightly lower, its height being 8,100 feet.

West of the divide and east of Snake River the country is mountainous, the summits ranging from 9,000 to 10,000 feet. There is little system to this country and the streams pursue circuitous courses. Snake River flows across the reserve in a course a little west of south in a marshy valley about a mile in width. The country west of Snake River is the northern extension of the Teton Range. It is here much depressed, presenting little of the rugged character which prevails farther south. On the southern border of the reserve these mountains reach an altitude of 9,000 feet, from which they descend to a depression at the north boundary of the reserve, where there is a broad pass connecting the valley of Snake River with Falls River Basin, and having at the divide an altitude of 7,000 feet. Falls River Basin, which occupies the western portion of the reserve, is low, level, and very marshy, with an altitude slightly less than 7,000 feet.

This region, owing to great altitude, has an ample rainfall and a severe climate. It is probable that no part of it is suitable for agriculture. The question of agricultural lands in this reserve may, therefore, be dismissed on account of the climate.

As a whole, this portion of the Yellowstone Park Reserve has much more forest on it than has the Teton Reserve, lying immediately south. This fact is largely due to the somewhat greater altitude of the region, and perhaps also to the fact that fires have not been quite so frequent or so destructive. There is no part of the reserve, except the limited areas which are above timber line, on which forests will not grow freely if protected from fires, and the fact that it is not entirely clothed with dense forests is probably due wholly to the former prevalence of this destructive agent.

The forests of this region are principally made up of *Pinus murrayana*, or lodge-pole pine. Besides this species groves of quaking aspen are scattered in many localities, especially where fires have raged in recent years. These are especially abundant west of the Teton range. In certain localities *Pinus flexilis* is found abundantly, especially about Huckleberry Peak, on the summit of the Continental Divide, and generally on exposed ridges. There is very little *Picea engelmanni* (Engelmann's spruce) in the reserve. It is found occasionally along the streams, and some is found about the slopes of the Continental Divide. Red fir is scattered about quite generally through the forests in isolated specimens. *Abies subalpina* is nowhere abundant, but is generally found on the higher elevations and along the streams. In brief, the species are the same as found in the Teton Reserve, and their distribution is similar. Indeed, the general notes relating to the Teton Reserve will be found to apply very closely to this one.

Since this reserve has not been subdivided, it will be necessary, in the detailed description of it, to refer to natural landmarks rather than to township lines. This description will be given, commencing at the east and going westward.

The valley of the Upper Yellowstone is, in the main, open or covered with willow brush. The lower slopes of the plateau to the east are pretty well timbered, especially on the isolated summit known as Hawks Rest, and the slopes of the valley of Thoroughfare Creek. The higher slopes and the summit of the plateau are entirely bare.

The northern end of the plateau, separating Atlantic Creek from Yellowstone River, is heavily timbered up to the summit. Following up the slopes of this plateau southward along the west wall of the valley of the Upper Yellowstone, the timber diminishes in amount and becomes reduced to scattered groves, which extend over the summit of the plateau, covering, perhaps, one-third its area. On the side toward Atlantic Creek this condition of things continues, but the proportion of land covered by the timber remains about the same. The valley of Atlantic Creek and the slopes of the plateaus rising from it on the west are covered with scattering groves of timber, one-fourth to one-half the land being covered. The plateau slopes rising from the valley of Falcon Creek on both sides are heavily timbered, but about the head of the creek the timber becomes scattering. The summit of the Continental Divide, from the north boundary of the reserve to Two Ocean Pass, is either bare or covered with scattered groves alternating with open parks.

West of the divide the country drained by the head waters of main Snake River and Fox Creek is covered with scattered groves of trees. Farther south, between Pacific and Mink creeks, upon the west slope of the divide, is found one of the heaviest bodies of timber in the reserve. It covers nearly 20 square miles, and is almost a solid forest, averaging over

2,000 feet B. M. to the acre. The central portion is the most dense, and there, for an area estimated at a square mile or more, the forests average more than 5,000 feet per acre. South of Pacific Creek is another considerable body of timber, averaging more than 2,000 feet per acre, although near the creek fire has destroyed some portions of it.

The east slopes of Big Game Ridge contain very little timber, distributed in groves. The west slope of the ridge is quite similar in timber distribution, except near its southern end. Here is another heavy body, covering most of the country between Gravel Creek and the summit of the ridge, an area 4 miles in length by 1 mile or more in breadth.

The country bordering on Harebell, Wolverine, and Coulter creeks contains scattered groves, the timber covering perhaps half the area. The timber becomes more dense farther down the course of main Coulter Creek. Southward, beyond the divide, along the streams flowing southward to Snake, there is very little timber. This region, extending on the north to the higher slopes of the hills and eastward as far as Pinon Peak and the valley of Gravel Creek, has apparently been burned not long ago, and some portions of it, as indicated by the red patches, very recently. On this area there are no large trees, but here and there are scattered groves alternating with barren patches. This incipient forest is mainly composed of firs and *Abies subalpina*. It contains also large areas of dead standing and fallen timber, the remains of the fires.

A large area of timber lies just east of Snake River, extending eastward north and south of Huckleberry Mountain. This consists mainly of dense groves of young Murray pines, interspersed here and there with dead standing timber, and on the higher elevations with *Pinus flexilis*.

West of Snake River the triangular area between the river and the stream leading up toward Grassy Lakes, on the north side, is covered with a scattering growth of pines of good size, suitable for lumber purposes. On the south side of this creek, extending across the divide and down the west side of the Teton Range, is a large area of good timber, grading above the 2,000-foot limit over most of the area, while in two localities about Grassy Lakes and on the west side of the divide it is still better, grading above 5,000 feet. Here and there throughout this body of timber are dead pines standing and fallen, giving evidence of fires in the past. A similar but smaller body of timber is seen on the south side of Berry Creek. On the higher summit of Teton Range the timber is either scattering or is entirely lacking.

SETTLEMENT.

The only settlement within this part of the reserve is a station of the United States troops on Snake River. There are no sawmills within it and it is unlikely that there will be any demand for timber from it in the immediate future, as the nearest settlements of magnitude, those in Teton Hole and in Wind River Valley, may be more economically supplied from other sources.

[Extract from annual report of Secretary of the Interior for fiscal year ended June 30, 1898.]

NATIONAL PARKS AND RESERVATIONS.

THE YELLOWSTONE NATIONAL PARK.

This is a tract of land near the head waters of the Yellowstone River, in the States of Montana and Wyoming, dedicated and set aside by the act of March 1, 1872 (17 Stat., 32), as a public park or pleasure ground for the benefit and enjoyment of the people. It is 62 miles in length from north to south, 54 miles in width from east to west, and contains about 3,348 square miles, or 2,142,720 acres. Its area is greater than that of the States of Delaware and Rhode Island combined. The average altitude is about 8,000 feet.

Capt. James B. Erwin, United States Army, the acting superintendent, reports that he assumed charge November 15, 1897, relieving Col. S. B. M. Young, United States Army, who had been ordered to active military duty, and has continued in charge since, except from March 13 to July 11, 1898, when he was on detached service, during which time Lieut. G. O. Cress, United States Army, performed the duties of superintendent.

During the winter of 1897-98 much vigilance was exercised on the part of the officers, men, and the scouts stationed in the park to protect the game from poachers, necessitating frequent trips on snowshoes to the sections of the park where the wild game is mostly to be found. Several poachers were arrested, subsequently convicted upon trial, and fined. Previous to June 1, at which date the stages begin their summer travel, crews were sent over all the roads, snow and fallen timber removed, and the roads otherwise repaired, making them safe for travel.

To meet the various demands of the public, different classes of transportation have been provided through the park, viz: Regular stage lines, steamboat transportation on Lake Yellowstone, licensed and private transportation, whether by wagon, pack train, horseback, or bicycle. The former is represented by the Yellowstone National Park Transportation Company, running its stages from Cinnabar, Mont., on the north of the park, the railroad terminus of a branch line of the Northern Pacific Railway, and over the usually traveled route of tourists, via Mammoth Hot Springs, Norris, Upper Geyser Basin, over the continental divide to Yellowstone Lake, Canyon, Norris, Mammoth Hot Springs, and thence to Cinnabar. The Mondia and Yellowstone Stage Company (Humphrey & Haynes) enter the park at Riverside, from Mondia, a station on the Oregon Short Line, and travel over the same route as the other stage line, as follows: Fountain Hotel, Upper Geyser Basin, over continental divide to Yellowstone Lake, Canyon, Norris, Mammoth Hot Springs, Norris, thence via Riverside to Mondia. The steamboat company operates one steamboat, which makes a daily trip on the lake. Licensed transportation includes a number of individuals who are licensed to personally conduct parties through the park, furnishing the necessary camp equipage and food.

The changes in the road system of the park during the past year and those contemplated for the coming year are as follows: The main traveled road, cut off Elk Park to Gibbon Meadow, is now completed and used by park transportation companies; the road along Madison River from falls of the Firehole River to boundaries of park completed and used by the Monida and Yellowstone Stage Company; road from Upper Geyser Basin to Lone Star Geyser is being used by the same company; road is projected from Canyon Hotel to Yancey's.

The total number of tourists visiting the park from opening of season (June 1) to September 30 was 6,534. The aggregate number carried over the regular route by the Yellowstone National Park Transportation Company was 2,196, and by the Monida and Yellowstone Stage Company 234; aggregate number carried through by licensed transportation of personally conducted camping parties, 890; aggregate number carried through in private transportation, 3,437; bicyclers, foot travelers, etc., included. During the season 2,256 tourists took the trip across Yellowstone Lake on the steamboat of the Yellowstone Lake Boat Company. Of this number, those who came into the park by the regular stage lines numbered 1,225, and those who went through the park by other means of transportation numbered 1,031.

The regulations for government of the park, established and enforced, though sometimes misunderstood and not appreciated by a few of the travelers of the park, seem to fully and completely accomplish the object for which the park was set aside, and the intentional violators of such rules and regulations of the park have been very few.

The system of enforcing them is by means of soldiers stationed at nearly regular distances on the usually traveled routes, who patrol same, and especially by guards from these stations, who are always present at the most interesting points, thereby preventing their desecration and the destruction of the natural phenomena. It has been in force for some years, and no better could be devised.

A complete and accurate record of all who enter and travel through the park is kept by the soldiers stationed at the various points in the reservation, except those who enter by the stage lines, a record of whom is kept at the hotels.

There has been no intentional violation of terms and conditions of any lease during the past year. During the season the Monida and Yellowstone Stage Company have constructed three barns, each holding from 8 to 12 horses, with additions for grain, and sleeping quarters for drivers and stock tenders.

The park has been exceptionally exempt from forest fires this year, due not only to the thoroughness with which the patrol work was done, but also to the growing carefulness in reference to fires exercised by camping parties and others. But two fires were reported, neither doing much damage, being brought under control by a detail of officers and men.

Leases held in the Yellowstone Park are as follows:

Yellowstone Park Transportation Company: Mammoth Hot Springs, 2 acres; Norris, 2 acres; Fountain, 1 acre; Upper Geyser Basin, 2 acres; Lake, 2 acres; Canyon, 1 acre, building, etc., for the accommodation of employees and stock.

Yellowstone Park Association: Mammoth Hot Springs, Mammoth Hotel and commissary; Mammoth Hot Springs, Cottage Hotel and Mammoth Barn; Fountain (Lower Basin), cottages; Fountain, Fountain Hotel and barn; Lake, Lake Hotel and barn; Canyon, Canyon Hotel, pump house, and barn; Upper Geyser Basin, hotel and barn (not yet constructed).

Yellowstone Lake Boat Company: Near Lake Hotel, 2 acres; Frank Island, 2 acres; Stevensons Island, 2 acres; Dot Island, 1 acre; West Thumb, 1 acre; Ways, 2 acres; Southeast Arm, 2 acres; Dot Island Game Corral, 2 acres; to be located by superintendent, 6 acres.

William W. Humphrey and F. Jay Haynes: At Upper Geyser Basin, Thumb, Lake Outlet, Grand Canyon, Norris Geyser Basin, Mammoth Hot Springs, not to exceed 1 acre at each point; building, etc., for the accommodation of employees and stock. (Assignments not yet made.)
Jennie H. Ash: Mammoth Hot Springs, dwelling, post-office, and store.
Ole A. Anderson: Mammoth Hot Springs, dwelling and store.
John F. Yancy: Pleasant Valley, hotel.
F. J. Haynes: Mammoth Hot Springs, studio; Upper Geyser Basin, studio.
Henry E. Klamer: Upper Geyser Basin, dwelling and store.

The Yellowstone Park Association owns and controls, under lease from the Department, hotels at the following places in the park: Mammoth Hot Springs, Lower Geyser Basin, Yellowstone Lake, and Canyon; also, lunch stations at Norris Geyser Basin, Upper Geyser Basin, and Yellowstone Lake. The hotels are all so located as to stage travel that tourists using this transportation always finish up their day's journey at a hotel, the lunch stations being merely places to obtain noonday refreshments en route. The hotels have been well conducted, but the association reports that the business has been carried on at a loss of about $25,000.

It asks to be relieved for the present of the responsibility of constructing a new and much-needed hotel at Upper Geyser Basin, which, under its lease of ground at that site, is to be completed in time for the tourist season next year. Frequent demands have been made for a hotel at this wonderful spot. Besides, by the erection of this hotel the present route through the park will be so divided up that much fatigue and discomfort to the tourist will be avoided.

Permanent camps were established during the year by W. W. Wylie, under contract with the Department, at the following points: Apollinaris Spring, Upper Geyser Basin, Yellowstone Lake, and Canyon, besides lunch stations at a point about midway between Norris and Lower Geyser Basin, near the Yellowstone Lake.

These camps seem to fulfill a demand on the part of a certain number of travelers in the park who wish to enjoy whatever benefits and pleasure may be received from camp life. Inspections made from time to time found them all neat and clean.

Frequent inspections have been made of all stage lines and other transportation, of the hotels, lunch stations, the permanent camps, and of the steamer on the Yellowstone Lake. The transportation lines have given excellent service to their patrons; their horses and vehicles are always in first-class condition and their personnel polite, courteous, and efficient. The hotels are thoroughly clean and neat, the food of the best quality and the service excellent, and fulfill every requirement of the traveling public. No complaints have been made.

The camps and lunch stations are neat and clean and have given satisfaction.

A number of trips were made on the steamer on Yellowstone Lake. It was always found to be in perfect condition and thoroughly safe.

Game in the park, excepting buffalo, is reported as increasing in numbers, and especially is this true of deer, elk, antelope, moose, and mountain sheep. Black bear are very plentiful and have proved very destructive to the stores of the troops on station, lunch stations, and campers. If they continue to increase in the future as in the past it will be necessary to take steps to rid the park of the yearly increase. They are numerous at the garbage piles of the hotels, and are objects of much interest and enjoyment to the tourists. The acting superintendent estimates that there are probably 50 buffalo yet in the park, and he attributes the fact that they are not increasing to too much interbreeding. He believes with new stock introduced into the herd an increase would follow. Coyotes are very numerous in certain sections, and they do some damage to the young elk, but the young deer and antelope are their particular prey. Beaver are more plentiful than ever before, and their locations are carefully watched and protected. Otter are abundant; martens plentiful; foxes are in goodly number, and there are many muskrats.

The many streams and lakes were largely stocked in the past with fish. The latter have multiplied, despite the enormous quantity caught yearly, and there is yet an abundant supply in all the streams.

The acting superintendent recommends the construction of a new road from the Canyon northward, following the canyon of the Yellowstone River, over Mount Washburn, and thence by way of Tower Creek to Yancey's, and thence to Mammoth Hot Springs. From the Canyon to Yancey's, by the eastern trail, the road will be about 23 miles long and can be built for $45,000.

From Yancey's to Mammoth Hot Springs is 20 miles. Some 4 or 5 miles of this road was built last year, leaving some 15 miles to construct, costing about $15,000, making $60,000 in all. The acting superintendent recommends that this amount be appropriated for this specific purpose in addition to the usual appropriation for the protection and improvement of the park. The construction of this road will obviate the necessity of visitors going over from 28 to 42 miles of the same road twice.

Appended to the report is a map of the park and forest reserve, showing the change in the road system since last year.

Under date of February 1, 1898, there was transmitted to Congress a report made on the 12th of January, 1898, by Col. S. B. M. Young, Third United States Cavalry, then acting superintendent of the park, recommending the extension of the limits of the park, and submitting a draft of a bill with a view to carrying the same into effect.

The boundaries, as suggested in said bill, which are indicated on a map accompanying the same, would extend the limits of the park so as to embrace the Yellowstone Timber Land Reserve, which lies on the east and south boundaries of the park and comprises about 1,914 square miles; all that portion of the Teton Forest Reserve lying east of the summit of the Teton Range and comprising about 1,050 square miles and adjoins the Yellowstone Timber Land Reserve on the south, together with an unreserved area of about 30 square miles at the southwest corner of the park in Idaho and an unreserved area of about 260 square miles at the northwest corner in Montana.

In the forest reserves are fine bodies of timber which it is important should be preserved from fires, because of its value as timber, as well as the protection to watersheds and against fires running into the park.

It is reported that during the winter months the large game from the national park herd roam, to a very considerable extent, in the areas proposed to be included within the park, and they should have all protection possible from destruction by marauders, who are constantly on the watch for game as it roams out of the park limits. The State game laws are applicable to the forest reserves, and for this reason it is impracticable to prevent the killing of game in the reserves in the same manner and to the same extent as it is prohibited in the park. The superior discipline of regular troops makes a more effective patrol than the civil forest officers; and cavalry can cover a greater extent of territory with more expedition and is better able to cope with trespassers than are forest rangers.

In view of the importance of protecting this country, which has an international reputation on account of its scenic beauties, and to throw additional safeguards about the big game whose natural home is the national park, and to protect more effectually the timber embraced in the forest reserves adjoining the park, I think it a wise policy that the additional areas herein described be embraced in and placed under the laws and management relating to the Yellowstone National Park.

Since the transmission of the bill hereinbefore referred to for the consideration of Congress petitions have been made to the Department by residents of the State of Wyoming in favor of including the portion of the timber-land reserve abutting Yellowstone Park on the south within the metes and bounds of the present Teton Forest Reserve, and the addition to the latter of certain public lands on the south frequented largely by game, and the creating therefrom of a new national park, to be managed separately from the Yellowstone.

The claims of Mr. Baronett, on account of a bridge built by him over the Yellowstone River, and those of Messrs. McCartney and McGuirk, respectively, for improvements made within the park prior to the act of dedication, are equitable and just, and payment of them should not be longer delayed. Recommendations have been made in the annual reports of my predecessors, as well as in my last annual report, that Congress make proper appropriation for the adjustment of their claims. These recommendations are renewed, as in my judgment all proprietary rights within the park should be removed.

[Extract from Appendix A, Report of the National Forestry Committee.]

3. The Teton Forest Reserve.

This proposed reserve embraces 829,440 acres, and is south of and adjacent to the Yellowstone Park Timber Land Reserve. The forests which cover it are similar in character to those in the Yellowstone National Park; they are capable of supplying all local demands that will probably ever be made on them, but have little commercial value. This proposed reserve contains the Teton Range of mountains and Jackson Lake, and some of the grandest and most picturesque scenery of the Rocky Mountains. Within its borders are many streams, flowing west, south, and north, and as a reservoir of moisture it is important.

Incidentally it may be mentioned that this proposed reserve is a favorite home of the elk and other large game, and that as a game reserve it would well supplement the Yellowstone National Park and the Yellowstone Park Timber Land Reserve. Within the proposed reserve only two quarter sections have been entered. A number of settlers, however, are living on unentered lands in the neighborhood of Jackson Lake.

TETON FOREST RESERVE.

SUMMARY.

Situation: Northwestern Wyoming.

	Acres.
Area within present lines	829,440
Adverse holdings not important.	
	Per cent of total area.
Area of forest land	65
Area marked by fire	'(?) 60
Area badly burned	(?) 40

Revised lines can not be drawn without further study.

Force recommended: This reserve should be provisionally placed in charge of the superintendent of Yellowstone National Park.

Sources of information: Report of T. S. Brandegee, special field assistant, United States Geological Survey. Statements of Henry Gannett, geographer, United States Geological Survey. No personal examination.

A rugged, broken mountain region, sparsely covered with open forest chiefly of lodge-pole pine, through which runs a broad valley of grazing land.

Injury from forest fires has been and continues to be very serious.

The protection of streams for irrigation is not of great importance here.

Mining has but little importance.

Agriculture is practiced little or not at all.

Grazing may probably be permitted in Jackson Hole.

Provision should be made to supply settlements in Jackson and Pierre holes with necessary lumber.

The Teton Forest Reserve is situated in northwestern Wyoming, contiguous to the Idaho boundary line, and has a length from east to west of 54 miles and a breadth from north to south of 24 miles. The total area included within its boundaries is 829,440 acres, nearly the whole of which is unburdened by adverse rights.

The striking feature of the topography is the Teton Range, which traverses the reserve from north to south and reaches an altitude of 13,370 feet. On the west the country descends rapidly to the valley of Pierre River and on the east to Jackson Hole. The latter is a level valley from 5 to 10 miles in width, crossing nearly the whole breadth of the reserve from north to south. It contains many lakes, the largest of which, Jackson Lake, is 10 miles long by 3 miles wide. The whole area of the reserve is drained by Snake River, which flows through Jackson Lake and Jackson Hole from north to south.

The climate is exceedingly severe, so much so that agriculture, except for the cultivation of forage plants, is said to be impossible. The rainfall, although no measurements have been made, is probably considerable, as would be indicated by the elevation, the mountainous character of the reserve, and the condition of the forest.

The forest.—The general character of the forest is broken and open. The trees are small, and the merchantable timber of the whole area trifling in amount compared with other reserves on the western slope of the continental divide. Four-fifths of the forest is composed of lodge-pole pine, with Engelmann spruce, Douglas fir (red fir), quaking aspen, and two cottonwoods as the other principal trees.

The lodge-pole pine is here a small tree, with average measurements as follows: Height, 60 feet; diameter, 1 foot; length of clear trunk, 25 feet. It is distributed from the lower portions of the reserve to an altitude of 9,000 feet, and furnishes fencing and rough building materials. The larger trees alone produce saw timber. The future economic value of the reserve must depend chiefly upon this tree.

The Englemann spruce occurs in moist situations from 7,000 to 10,000 feet in altitude, chiefly near the streams. It is abundant in places, and furnishes the larger proportion of logs cut in the reserve. Its average measurements are as follows: Height, 100 feet; diameter, 2 feet; length of clear trunk, none.

The Douglas fir (red fir) is not a common tree, nor anywhere locally abundant. It occupies for the most part dry situations, and resists fire exceedingly well. The average dimensions of mature trees are as follows: Height, 80 feet; diameter, 2 feet; length of clear trunk, 15 feet.

The quaking aspen and two cottonwoods are abundant, but for the present not economically important. The quaking aspen is next in abundance to the lodge-pole pine, and has approximately the same distribution, while the cottonwoods occur chiefly along streams. The latter occasionally reach a diameter of 4 feet, with a height of 75 feet.

Fire.—The whole area of the reserve is said to have been repeatedly burned over, with great damage to the forest. The inflammable character of its principal tree, the lodge-pole pine, here gives the fire question striking importance, as it does wherever this tree forms a considerable element of the forest growth.

Water.—Since the reserve contains only grazing and forest lands, irrigation, which has hitherto assumed no importance, is not expected to develop to any marked extent in the future.

Mining.—There has been no mining development of consequence within the reserve.

Agriculture.—As has been indicated, agriculture is without importance in this reserve, and no measures need be taken with a view to its extension in the near future.

Grazing.—Many thousand acres of grazing land are included in Jackson Hole, and some provision will be required to regulate pasturage, unless it is decided to exclude this area from the reserve. Since I am not personally acquainted with this reserve I am not prepared to make a specific recommendation upon the subject.

Forest force.—I am not prepared to make specific recommendations. The extent and situation of the reserve appear to indicate that it should be provisionally assimilated to the Yellowstone Park Forest Reserve. In that case special regulations will be required to open the reserve itself and all its resources to conservative use.

Forest management.—The present source of demand for the timber of the reserve are the settlements in Jackson and Pierre holes. The poor quality of the timber makes it certain that no large trade in forest produce can be developed within the reserve for some time to come, but eventually water transportation by way of the Snake River and its larger tributaries will make this forest economically important for the less thoroughly timbered regions down the river.

REPORT

OF THE

ACTING SUPERINTENDENT OF THE YELLOWSTONE NATIONAL PARK.

DEPARTMENT OF INTERIOR,
YELLOWSTONE NATIONAL PARK,
OFFICE OF THE SUPERINTENDENT,
Mammoth Hot Springs, Wyo., September 30, 1898.

SIR: I have the honor to submit the following report of the condition, management, protection, and improvement of the Yellowstone National Park from November 10, 1897, the date of the final report of my predecessor, to September 30, 1898:

Maj. Gen. S. B. M. Young, United States Volunteers (Colonel Third Cavalry, acting superintendent), left the Yellowstone National Park on November 15, 1897, and the duties of that position have devolved upon me, as being next in command, and subsequently, in compliance with telegraphic orders from the Department, from that time to the present, except during the period from March 13 to July 11, 1898, when I was on detached service, during which time Lieut. G. O. Cress, Fourth Cavalry, ably performed these duties.

At the time of departure of my predecessor there remained an unexpended balance of $66.01, with which to keep in repair the road from the Mammoth Hot Springs to Gardiner City, which, on account of its location in the canyon of the Gardiner River, must be constantly worked in the winter season; to protect the game of the park during the winter months from poachers; to open up the usually traveled route of tourists, who begin visiting the park on the 1st of June, and keep the same in repair until the appropriation for this year should become available. Owing to the very small balance of the appropriation remaining unexpended I had to rely mainly for protecting the game upon the services of Lieutenant Lindsley, Fourth Cavalry, and Scouts Morrison and Whittaker, with the assistance of the soldiers on winter station and in garrison. The work done by this officer, and these men, was of the highest importance to the park in the protection of its game, to a large extent prevented poaching, and resulted, in connection with the mild weather of last winter, in a large increase of the game life of all descriptions. The way in which these objects were accomplished will be treated under the heads of "Protection" and "Improvement" later on in this report.

The stage robbery which occurred in the park on August 14, 1897, an account of which was given by my predecessor in his report, was brought to an end by the trial and conviction of George Reeb and Gus. Smitzer, at Cheyenne, Wyo., before United States court, and they were sentenced to two and one-half years in the penitentiary.

TRAVEL.

To supply the various demands of the public for transportation through the park, it has been found necessary to have and adopt different kinds, viz: Regular stage lines, steamboat transportation on Lake Yellowstone, licensed, and private transportation, whether by wagon, pack train, horseback, or bicycle. The former is represented by the Yellowstone National Park Transportation Company, running its stages from Cinnabar, Mont., on the north of the park, the railroad terminus of a branch line of the Northern Pacific Railway, and over the usually traveled route of tourists, via Mammoth Hot Springs, Norris, Upper Geyser Basin, over the continental divide to Yellowstone Lake, Canyon, Norris, Mammoth Hot Springs, and thence to Cinnabar. The Monida and Yellowstone Stage Company (Humphrey & Haynes) enter the park at Riverside, from Monida, a station on the Oregon Short Line, and travel over the same route as the other stage line, as follows: Fountain Hotel, Upper Geyser Basin, over continental divide to Yellowstone Lake, Canyon, Norris, Mammoth Hot Springs, Norris, thence via Riverside to Monida.

The steamboat company operates one steamboat, which daily makes the trip from the lunch station on the lake (known as West Thumb) to the Lake Hotel, and affords the tourist, whatever means of transportation he may use in making the park trip, an opportunity to take an exceedingly beautiful and interesting trip of some three hours on the lake.

Licensed transportation includes a number of individuals, who, under license from the Department, are authorized to personally conduct parties through the park, furnishing the necessary camp equipage and food. Private transportation, as its name implies, includes all other going through the park, using transportation of their own, of whatever nature.

For the purposes of protection and police, it has been found necessary to register at certain places in the park all persons traveling through it, exclusive of those transported by the regular stage lines, and below will be found a table giving the number of travelers in the park this year and the kind of transportation used.

Number of persons registered at stations during the season of 1898.

Number and location of station.	Camping parties.				Licensed transportation.			
	June.	July.	Aug.	Sept.	June.	July.	Aug.	Sept.
1. Mammoth Hot Springs	241	512	1,174	256	66	166	352	65
2. Norris *a b*								
3. Canyon *a*								
4. Lake *b*	71	538	1,263	469	42	112	240	30
5. Thumb *a*								
6. Upper Basin	25	436	1,212	471	9	70	295	58
7. Lower Basin *b*	77	390	1,327	423	17	73	428	61
8. Snake River *b*	24	210	557	219			None.	
9. Riverside *b*	88	366	911		19	55	88	
10. Soda Butte *b*	99	162	170	114			None.	

a No registration required.
b Winter station.

Number of persons traveling with registered guides (pack trains).

June	None.
July	39
August	74
September	31

The aggregate number of tourists visiting the park from opening of season (June 1) to September 30 was 6,534. The aggregate number carried over the regular route by the Yellowstone National Park Transportation Company, was 2,196, and by the Monida and Yellowstone Stage Company, 234; aggregate number carried through by licensed transportation of personally conducted camping parties, 890; aggregate number carried through in private transportation, 3,437; bicyclers, foot travelers, etc., included. During the season 2,256 tourists took the trip across Yellowstone Lake on the steamboat of the Yellowstone Lake Boat Company. Of this number, those who came into the park by the regular stage lines numbered 1,225, and those who went through the park by other means of transportation numbered 1,031.

To determine whether or not the park is becoming more traveled, and fulfilling gradually the mission for which created, viz, as a "pleasuring ground for the benefit and enjoyment of the people", a comparison of totals is made, from record, from 1895 to present date:

Number of tourists former years.

	1895.	1896.	1897.	1898.
Camping parties	2,594	1,797	4,454	3,437
Licensed transportation	374	454	1,354	890
Yellowstone Park Association	2,470	2,408	4,872	2,207
Total	5,438	4,659	10,680	6,534

It will be seen that 1897 brought the greatest number of tourists to the park, but the comparison should not be made with that year as a standard, as a great number of Christian Endeavorers, after their meeting in San Francisco, Cal., returned, via the Northern Pacific Railway, and visited the park. Their number can not be determined, but making reasonable deductions on account of this particular and exceptional class of travel, it will be seen that the season of 1898 in the park shows an increased number of tourists. This is yet more remarkable, as the conditions of the country, owing to the war, diverted more or less attention from the park, and probably decreased in no inconsiderable degree the number of persons traveling for pleasure during the summer.

SYSTEM OF PATROLING AND POLICING.

The most difficult task that the acting superintendent has to accomplish is to carry out the provisions of the dedicatory act of the park, setting it aside for the benefit and enjoyment of the people. Were it thrown open to the people, without restrictions of any sort, it would be only a short time before it would cease to be a pleasuring ground, while, on the other hand, the restrictions should be of such a nature only as to preserve intact, not only for the present but for the future, the salient and wonderful features which have made the park the most remarkable, as well as the most scientifically interesting, place in the world. The restrictions, as now established and sanctioned by the Interior Department, and enforced by the acting superintendent of the park through the military force under his command, though sometimes misunderstood and not appreciated by a few of the travelers of the park, seem to fully and completely accomplish the object for which the park was set aside, and I am glad to say the intentional violators of the rules and regulations of the park have been very few.

The system of enforcing them by means of soldiers stationed at nearly regular distances on the usually traveled routes, and who patrol these routes, and especially by guards from these detachments, who are always present at the most interesting points, preventing their desecration and the destruction of the natural phenomena, has been established for some years, and no better could be devised. I know of no case where these soldiers, in the discharge of these very particular and exacting duties, have been other than courteous and polite toward the public, at the same time enforcing the law. These rules and regulations will be found in the appendix marked A.

In addition to these duties, it has been found necessary to keep a complete and accurate record of all who enter and travel through the park, except those who enter by the stage lines, a record of whom is kept at hotels, and this is also done by the soldiers stationed at the various points in the park.

HOTELS.

The Yellowstone Park Association owns and controls, under lease from the Department, hotels at the following places in the park: Mammoth Hot Springs, Lower Geyser Basin, Yellowstone Lake, Canyon; also lunch stations at Norris Geyser Basin, Upper Geyser Basin, and Yellowstone Lake. The hotels are so located as to stage travel that tourists using this transportation always finish up their day's journey at a hotel; the lunch stations being merely places to obtain noonday refreshments en route to hotels. It is, I believe, the intention of the association to build a hotel at the Upper Geyser Basin this fall. I trust this will be done, and completed in time for the tourist season of next year. Frequent demands have been made for a hotel at this most wonderful spot; besides, by the erection of this hotel, the present route through the park will be so divided up that much fatigue and discomfort to the tourist will be avoided.

PERMANENT CAMPS.

Under authority from the Department, Mr. W. W. Wylie has established permanent camps at the following points: Apollinaris Spring, Upper Geyser Basin, Yellowstone Lake, and Canyon, besides having lunch stations at a point about midway between Norris and Lower Geyser Basin, and near the Yellowstone Lake.

INSPECTION BY ACTING SUPERINTENDENT OF THE PARK.

Ever since the opening of the season, and until its close, frequent inspections have been made by me and other officers of the command, of all stage lines and other transportation, of the hotels, lunch stations, and of Mr. Wylie's permanent camps and lunch stations, and of the steamer on the Yellowstone Lake.

I have always found the entire personnel of the Yellowstone National Park Transportation Company polite, courteous, and efficient; their horses and vehicles always in first-class condition, and suited in every way to handle the business required of it.

The Monida and Yellowstone Stage Company is in the first year of its existence, and has employed the following:

Four-horse drivers	10–12
Two-horse drivers	4
Stock tenders	7
Assistant superintendents	2
Blacksmith	1
Bookkeeper	1

They had in use the following vehicles:

Eleven-passenger Concord coaches	12
Three-passenger Concord surries	4
Concord buggies	2

Also:

Horses	80
Four-horse Concord harness ...sets	16
Two-horse Concord harness ...do	8
Blankets, dusters, and complete barn supplies.	

This stage company is of the first order in every respect; has given first-class service to its patrons, has opened up a new route to the park through a beautiful country, and I have found its entire personnel, by courtesy and politeness, desirous of making its route popular with the traveling public, which it will undoubtedly be.

Messrs. Humphrey & Haynes, who control the line, are both practical business men, with experience in this business, and are always courteous and obliging.

The steamer *Zillah*, running daily trips on the Yellowstone Lake, under the lease of the Lake Boat Company, and under the personal direction of Mr. E. C. Waters, her captain, who is also president and general manager of the company, has given full satisfaction to the public. I have made many trips on this boat, always found her in perfect condition, and thoroughly safe. The entire personnel of the boat are always attentive and polite to the passengers, doing everything for their pleasure and enjoyment. In addition to the regular tourist business, this steamer has had many excursions.

The hotels and lunch stations of the Yellowstone Park Association, under the able direction and management of Mr. J. H. Dean, fulfill every requirement of the traveling public. No better accommodations and food are furnished anywhere in the United States, under like conditions. The hotels are thoroughly clean and neat throughout, and the service excellent. It should be remembered that all articles of food, except meat, are shipped here, as there is no local market from which the daily supply of edibles can be obtained. I have not heard a single complaint from any guest of any of the hotels.

The permanent camps of Mr. W. W. Wylie seem to fulfill a demand on the part of a certain number of travelers in the park who wish to enjoy whatever benefits and pleasures may be received from camp life. I inspected frequently each of his camps and lunch stations, and found them all neat and clean, with all the comforts one could expect to find in camp. It is not possible to make a comparison between the accommodations furnished by these camps and the hotels. Each comes fully up to the requirements of its especial class, and the personal preference of each visitor to the park must and will determine the way of living while in the park.

Campers are another class of visitors to the park who furnish their own transportation, tentage, etc., and with whom the daily patrols from stations have most to do in reference to the police and protection of the park.

The transportation under the heading "Licensed" has also been inspected and the camps of these parties looked after, wherever met. Satisfaction seems to have been given in all cases, for I have not heard one word of complaint from any of their patrons. A list of this licensed transportation will be found in the appendix marked B.

With private transportation of all sorts and descriptions the Department is not interested, except pack-mule transportation. Certain rules govern this kind while in the park, rendered necessary by a due regard to the safety of others traveling in vehicles, as well as the safety of the parties using the pack mules. This is the kind of transportation that is most generally used by hunting parties in the fall of the year, wishing to go through the park and hunt in the country south, southeast, and southwest of the park. Such transportation is restricted to the conditions of traveling on the usually traveled roads and leading the pack animals, for the reasons given above. When the party is under the control of a registered guide a greater latitude is allowed to the routes taken through the park, and a guide is only registered when he is personally known to be absolutely competent and reliable. A list of these registered guides will be found in the appendix marked C.

The Monida and Yellowstone Stage Company have seemingly absorbed the business previously conducted by Mr. C. J. Bassett, from Beaver Canyon, Idaho, into the park via the western entrance, as I have no reports of any passengers by his line during the past season, nor has he applied for license to conduct this class of business.

CARRYING FIREARMS THROUGH THE PARK.

The custom of carrying firearms of some description is nearly universal among the citizens of States bordering the park, who travel in their own conveyances, or on saddle animals; and of course those desiring to hunt in the country adjacent to the park, and who go through the park either on starting on their trip or returning, are fully equipped in this particular. With reference to all of these individuals, the regulation prohibiting firearms in the park, except on written permission from the acting superintendent, in which case the arms are sealed, has been strictly enforced. It is a wise regulation, and its enforcement is essential to the protection of the park.

The mere fact that this region has been set aside as a national park engenders a feeling of hostility toward it and toward the authorities here, on the part of the people living nearest to it; and the fact that it abounds in game, which is becoming more and more rare in other parts of the United States, intensifies the feeling of enmity. As the benefits to the people of the surrounding country derived from keeping the park intact and the game protected become better understood by them, this hostility will undoubtedly cease; and in performing the duties of acting superintendent I have endeavored to make this plain to all I have been brought in contact with, and, so far as possible, to make them friends of the park.

LEASES.

There has been no intentional violation of terms and conditions of any lease during the past year. The rentals under these leases are paid direct to the Department in Washington, except that of Mrs. Jennie H. Ash, which was forwarded through this office under date of August 9, 1898, and its receipt duly acknowledged.

The Monida and Yellowstone Stage Company have constructed on sites selected by me, three neat barns, holding from 8 to 12 horses (one at Upper Geyser Basin, 8 horses; one at Norris Geyser Basin, 12 horses; one at Mammoth Hot Springs, 12 horses), with additions for grain and sleeping quarters for drivers and stock tenders.

At the Fountain, Lake, and Grand Canyon they have used the barns of the Yellowstone Park Association; having made such arrangements until locations are made and permanent barns constructed.

The railway station of this line is Monida, on the Oregon Short Line, 60 miles west from the west entrance to the park ("Dwelles").

Between Dwelles and Monida is operated a daily relay line, and in use on this daily are 32 horses and 2 extra coaches. These extra coaches have been kept at Monida in case more tourists applied than could be accommodated by the daily.

At Dwelles are kept 7 coaches and 3 surreys, with drivers and teams, for park service. At Norris are kept 1 coach and 1 surrey to accommodate tourists holding Northern Pacific tickets, "Norris to Monida", who have made the regular park trip and are ticketed out via Monida. These are picked up at Norris, taken to Dwelles for the night, and then take the daily to Monida the following day.

A barn has been constructed at Monida that will accommodate 20 horses, and wagon sheds to accommodate the entire outfit. Wagons, harness, and equipment will be placed in the Monida barn for the winter and $20,000 insurance placed on same. Horses will be wintered in the lower Centennial Valley.

Stations have been constructed at Reeds, Red Rock Pass (Klondyke), and at Dwelles. A wagon bridge has been constructed by this company over the south fork of the Madison River, costing $75; approaches have been built to the Snake River ford, and a crew of 3 men and 1 team have been employed for two months, keeping the road free of rock and in repair.

Madison County appropriated $500, which was expended in addition upon the road between Monida and Dwelles. This road is now far better than the ordinary country road, and is nearly as good as the roads within the park. I append stage schedule of this company (Appendix G). The plats of the various sites granted under and required by lease from the Department to this company will be forwarded as soon as completed.

The building of Mr. H. E. Klamer, at Upper Geyser Basin, referred to in last year's report as not being then received, has been completed and received. A list of leases now held in the park is hereto appended (Appendix D).

UNITED STATES COMMISSIONER AND HIS WORK.

The presence of a United States commissioner at Mammoth Hot Springs to hear and determine cases of violations of the park laws and regulations is eminently satisfactory, and continues to do much to prevent these violations. I append herewith a report of persons tried by him (Appendix E).

FIRES.

The park has been exceptionally exempt from forest fires this year, due not only to the thoroughness with which the patrol work was done, but also to the growing carefulness in reference to fires exercised by camping parties and others. On August 8 a fire was reported 9 miles northwest of Riverside Station, a short distance outside the park limits, but as the direction of the prevailing wind would soon bring it within the park, a detail of officers and men were sent, and after two days of much fatigue and hard work it was brought under control.

On August 26 a fire was reported and located between Barlow's Fork and Heart River in the southeastern portion of the park, but fortunately rain followed for several days, extinguishing it and rendering no work on the part of the troops necessary, other than a careful watch for several days. The causes of neither of these fires could be definitely determined, but that of August 26 unquestionably originated from camp fires carelessly left burning or smoldering. The origin of the fire of August 8 was not so plainly accidental, and the inquiry as to its origin was limited to the determination that its starting point was not within the park limits. It ought not to be difficult for campers in and in the vicinity of the park to understand the incalculable damage, both in the present and for future years, that can be done by not carefully complying with the park laws in this respect.

FOREST RESERVES.

Bordering on the eastern and southern limits of the park are two forest reserves, both of which have been recommended by my predecessor to be brought within the park boundaries and made a part thereof. It will be remembered that these tracts of land were set aside and established as a public reservation by proclamation of the President, made on March 30 and September 10, 1891, and though not coming within the provisions of the act of Congress approved May 7, 1894, are yet under the jurisdiction and control of the acting superintendent and the military force in the park for the enforcement of the law setting them aside, especially relating to the preservation of the game. To thoroughly determine the character of the forest reserve on the east, the settlers therein, game, etc., Lieutenant Lindsley, Fourth Cavalry, was sent to investigate the same, and on his return submitted a report which will be found in the appendix (F). It will be seen that there are many settlers in it, some in violation of law, and that a few mining claims are being worked.

The country does not seem to be the habitat of any large quantity of game. The forest reserve on the south contains no settlers, is of no mineral value, and is unquestionably a game country. I would for these reasons, therefore, urge that the forest reserve on the south be made a part of the park, and the forest reserve on the east be not further considered with this end in view. It is probable that whatever opposition has hitherto been encountered in taking in both of these reserves as part of the park would cease, when it is proposed to take in only that one on the south, which possesses only the advantage of being a great game country, and has no mineral or agricultural advantage to settlers. I would also recommend that the necessary legislation be enacted, bringing the forest reserves bordering the park under the provision of the National Park protective act, approved May 7, 1894, to preserve and protect the game. As is set forth in the notice of the Department, which has been placed in conspicuous places in and about the park, "All persons are warned not to hunt nor kill game thereon", and the penalty for doing this is ejection from the reserve, prosecution for trespass, and the holding of such persons pecuniarily responsible for any waste or damage, whether done intentionally or caused by neglect. Such is the extent of the punishment, and in its present mild form it does not form a sufficient safeguard for the protection of the reserve and its game.

PROTECTION.

The following animals are found in the park:

Antelope.—These are yet numerous. The snow drives them from the mountains and high plateaus, their feeding and breeding ground in spring and summer, to the lower altitudes outside of the park, where many are killed.

Bear.—Plentiful, and have proved destructive to the stores of the detachments on station, lunch stations, and campers. If they continue to increase in the future as in the past, some means will have to be taken to rid the park of the yearly increase. They are numerous at the garbage piles of the hotels, and are objects of much interest and enjoyment to the tourists.

Buffalo.—There are probably 50 of these animals yet in the park. They are not increasing—due, I believe, to too much inbreeding. This is about the only wild herd in the United States, and steps should be taken to prevent the extermination of this herd from the evils of inbreeding by the purchase of a few good bulls. Full and ample protection is given these animals, and I believe that with new stock introduced into the herd, an increase would follow.

Coyotes.—Very numerous in certain sections. They do some damage to the young elk, but the young deer and antelope are their particular prey. Efforts are made in winter to keep their number down by poisoning carcasses of dead animals, and to a certain extent it has been successful.

Deer.—Numerous, on the increase; and the protection afforded them has done much to make them very tame. They are frequently seen by tourists along the usually traveled route.

Elk.—Numerous, and are increasing. The park is their breeding place in spring, and feeding ground in winter. Immense herds can be seen in nearly any direction in winter, and in certain localities in summer.

Fur-bearing animals.—Beaver, more plentiful than ever before, and their locations in the various streams in the park are carefully watched and protected. Numerous new dams have been constructed. Otter are fairly abundant. Martens are plentiful and widely distributed as are also the Canadian lynx, wild-cat, and mink. Foxes are in goodly number, the black and red being frequently seen, and some timber foxes being reported. There are also some badgers, and a great many muskrats, ground hogs, squirrels, chipmunks, skunks, porcupines, and rabbits. Of the latter there are the cottontails, a few jack-rabbits, many snowshoe rabbits, and the paca, the tiny rock rabbit. All these animals are increasing yearly.

Moose.—Quite numerous in the south and southwestern portions of the park and forest reserve, and are apparently increasing.

Sheep.—In considerable numbers in various sections of the park; especially are they conspicuous in winter, when they leave the higher peaks and seek a somewhat lower level to feed, and later on to breed. I believe their number is increasing.

Wolverines.—While not plentiful are distributed over a large area of the park.

BIRDS.

Pelicans, geese, ducks, gulls, cranes, swans, ospreys, hawks, eagles, grouse, jays of all kinds, water ousel, robins, kingfishers, and various other small birds abound in the park. The aquatic birds nest here and remain here until late in the fall, and, it is probable, during the winter in streams and lakes where the hot springs prevent entire freezing of the water.

As already stated, at the opening of the winter there was but a balance of $66.01 remaining on hand for both the protection and improvement. Using this until exhausted, and relying upon the untiring efforts and conscientious work of Lieutenant Lindsley, soldiers, and a volunteer scout, the protection of the park was as efficiently performed, if not to a greater extent, than in former years. The plan adopted was to ascertain the location of all persons who in past years have been guilty, or thought guilty of poaching, and never let them get beyond the surveillance of the park authorities. This was successfully done in many cases, and resulted in the capture and trial of some of them by the United States commissioner; and, with the assistance of the State authorities, by the civil courts, thus deterring others from attempting to poach. Unless actually taking part in the winter work here, the hardships are inconceivable, and I forward herewith as an appendix the report of these trips made by scouts and others, showing the work done. It represents miles of snowshoeing, embracing all portions of the park, under all sorts of weather and temperature, where the parties were their own pack animals, camping usually where night found them, or resorting to the snowshoe shacks, affording but little protection.

The Department supplied sleeping bags, which are of incalculable comfort; and before the winter sets in, comfortable cabins will be built at necessary and convenient points, stocked with rations and bedding, and having stoves, which will lessen materially the hardships and discomforts of these trips. With the end in view of having transportation of some sort for necessary articles for these winter scouting parties, I believed that the reindeer recently purchased by the Government for the Klondike relief party, which was subsequently abandoned, could be used to advantage, and accordingly addressed a letter to the Department asking, if practicable, that a few be sent here for this purpose. It is unfortunate that these animals were so located that they could not be sent here, for in the use of these animals or in sledge dogs lies the solution of winter work in the park.

FISH.

Many streams and lakes were stocked in 1889, 1890, 1893, and 1895, have multiplied abundantly, and in spite of the enormous quantity caught yearly, and those destroyed by animals and birds, there is apparently an ample quantity yet in all the streams. I endeavored to have a hatchery established in the park, believing this to be the most appropriate and suitable place in the United States, as this is the reservoir drained by the principal rivers of the Atlantic and Pacific oceans, and fish planted in these streams would, with natural conditions fulfilled, soon fill the streams outside the park, but the United States Fish Commission did not deem it advisable. Later on this year, it is my intention to determine if the lake bass planted in certain lakes in the park have survived; none as yet have been caught, and it is possible that they may have perished for want of proper food. There are certain waters in the park that will afford ample food for them, and, if possible, these waters will be stocked. There is no finer trout fishing in the world than that of the waters of the park, and it is free to all.

From the above it will be seen that the park as a game and fish preserve has not its equal in the world; the variety is great, and it is eminently fitted to sustain this variety under the protection of the Government. An increase in appropriation means an increase in the means and facilities of protection, and as a national game preserve, which not only holds secure the remaining wild animals and game birds of this country, but enables them to breed and multiply, thus supplying the needs of neighboring States, it is deserving of an increased fund for this purpose. This leaves out entirely its charm as a pleasure ground for the tourist, with its wonderful natural phenomena. To maintain both of these conditions there is but one inadequate appropriation for the park, viz, that for its protection and improvement.

IMPROVEMENT.

Nature can not be improved upon; the wise policy for years held by the various acting superintendents, has resulted in the laying out of roads interfering the least with natural conditions, and affording the sight-seer with the easiest, most direct, and at the same time safest routes to those wonderful sights which nature has lavishly worked in the park. This work is not yet completed, and some of the grandest scenery and phenomena in the park are yet unseen by the great majority of visitors, on account of lack of means to construct these safe and convenient roads. The first work in the spring, previous to June 1, at which date the stages begin their summer travel, is to send a crew over all the roads, shoveling out snow yet remaining in deep drifts in many places, removing fallen timber, repairing the roads, and making them safe and fit for traveling. As stated before in this report, there were absolutely no funds on hand for this work at the opening of the present season, but with the aid of the scouts and soldiers the roads were opened up, and put in fit condition for travel, and no delay was caused to the tourists.

As is well known, the present traveled route carries the tourist from Cinnabar, via Mammoth Hot Springs, Norris Geyser Basin, Lower Geyser Basin, Upper Geyser Basin, Lake, Canyon, and again to Norris, Mammoth Hot Springs, to Cinnabar; or, arriving at Monida, he enters the park on it western boundary at Riverside, thence to Lower Geyser Basin, and with the exception of the ride from Mammoth Hot Springs to Cinnabar, his route is as above, returning to Monida via Riverside. It is thus seen that 28 miles in one case, and 42 miles in the other is gone over twice, which is objectionable. This can be avoided by the construction of a road from the canyon northward, following the canyon of the Yellowstone River over Mount Washburn, and thence by way of Tower Creek into Yancey's, and thence into the Mammoth Hot Springs.

There are at present two trails leading from the canyon to Yancey's over Mount Washburn, joining about a mile and a half south of Tower Creek. I have been over both of these trails, examining each carefully, both for scenic effect and practicability for road construction, and on both these grounds am thoroughly satisfied that the eastern (or lower) trail is the route to be followed in constructing this road, which will be about 23 miles long, and can be built for $45,000. From Yancey's to Mammoth Hot Springs is 20 miles. Some 4 or 5 miles of the most costly part of this road was built last year, and has been kept in thoroughly first-class condition, leaving some 15 miles to construct, costing about $15,000. It is recommended that this amount ($60,000) be appropriated for this specific purpose, in addition to the usual annual appropriation for the protection and improvement of the park.

The monthly reports of work done in the improvement of the park have given in detail what has been accomplished the past summer, and the further projected improvement in roads already constructed, as set forth in project submitted at the time the appropriation became available, will be completed before the close of the season.

This will be done within the limits of the appropriation, still keeping sufficient on hand for the protection of the park during the eight months of winter, and for opening the roads for tourist travel beginning on the 1st of next June. Taking out of the appropriation for this year of $40,000 the smallest necessary amount for protection ($3,000), there remains but $37,000 with which to do this work. And when it is remembered there is 170 miles of constructed road which has to be gone over entirely at the commencement of every season, kept in repair for four months of the year, and then put in the best possible shape to withstand the effects of winter, it must be confessed that $218 is but a scant allowance for each mile of road. I have not the data available to make the comparison, but I doubt if there is any road in the country which is traveled so much by the public, demanding a good road, which costs so little per mile. Here is also seen the impossibility of yielding to the demands of the tourists for more new roads leading to places of interest and beauty reached now only by trails, and not to be carried over twice some portion of the route now used. The amount now appropriated is the smallest amount with which the protection and present road condition in the park can be maintained, and if Congress intends to ratify and make good its dedication of the park to the people of the United States as a pleasuring ground for its benefit and enjoyment, it should yield to the demands of the people and make additional appropriation for the construction of new roads, which will add to their pleasure and benefit by opening new and wonderful phenomena and scenery.

NATURAL PHENOMENA OF THE PARK.

There does not seem to be any material change in these during the past year. Certain geysers and hot springs are noted as having become extinct, and others which were quiescent have again become active. The geysers which can be depended upon for regular displays are few in numbers, but constant observation of nearly all of them has enabled their time of eruption to be determined with sufficient accuracy to inform tourists, and give them an opportunity to witness their marvelous displays. There is unquestionably a close connection between temperature of water in the geyser and its time of eruption, certain geysers erupting when the water in their craters reaches a certain temperature, which varies for each geyser, and with the proper instruments for taking temperatures it will not be difficult to foretell the time of display of those geysers which are of greatest celebrity, and thus afford tourists the opportunity of seeing them. I will, if possible, determine the eruptive temperature of the most important geysers before the next tourist season, and will be enabled to give due notice of their eruption.

Mud Geyser has been exceedingly active for a period of two weeks this summer. It has for some years been a somewhat quiescent, boiling mud pool, but in the latter part of July it became more violent, and soon gave a remarkable display of its powers, throwing immense clots of mud 50 and 100 feet away from its crater. It covered the ground and trees in its vicinity and was in this state of eruption for two weeks. It gradually became quiet, but the contents of its crater have changed from boiling mud to boiling dirty water. The Black Growler, in Norris Basin, has also displayed remarkable activite this summer, and the noise of the escaping steam through its crater could be heard for miles; and at the base a mud spring has broken forth, which apparently seems to be growing larger. The Constant Geyser has within the past three weeks ceased to play, after many years of uninterrupted activity.

A new road, now completed, between Elk Park and Gibbon Meadow, on the road from Norris to Fountain, leads past two beautiful chocolate-colored geysers situated on opposite sides of the Gibbon River. They are immense cones. From the top of each a goodly stream of water continually boils and is ejected some feet in the air. The cascades and rapids along the road, which follows the river, are exceedingly picturesque and beautiful.

I forward herewith a map of the park and forest reserve, the same that accompanied the report of last year of the acting superintendent. Upon this I have marked the changes in road system of the park. They are as follows:

Main traveled road, cut off Elk Park to Gibbon Meadow, now notated as completed and used by park transportation companies; road along Madison River from falls of the Firehole River to boundaries of park completed and used by the Monida and Yellowstone Stage Company; road from Upper Geyser Basin to Lone Star Geyser, notated as being used by the same company; projected road from Canyon Hotel to Yancey's, notated so as to show the lower (or eastern) trail as the one recommended to be built, instead of the upper (or western) trail as shown on the map.

My efforts to preserve and maintain the park intact, and for its protection and improvement have been ably seconded by all officers of this command.

Supplementary reports will be submitted at the close of the season, when the weather prevents further work on the roads, and at such times during the coming winter as will keep the Department fully informed of the condition of affairs in the park.

I submit herewith the meteorological record as kept at Fort Yellowstone by the post surgeon.

Very respectfully,

JAMES B. ERWIN,
Captain, Fourth Cavalry, Acting Superintendent.

The SECRETARY OF THE INTERIOR,
Washington, D. C.

APPENDIX A.

RULES AND REGULATIONS OF THE YELLOWSTONE NATIONAL PARK.

DEPARTMENT OF THE INTERIOR,
Washington, D. C., June 1, 1897.

The following rules and regulations for the government of the Yellowstone National Park are hereby established and made public pursuant to authority conferred by section 2475, Revised Statutes United States, and the act of Congress approved May 7, 1894:

1. It is forbidden to remove or injure the sediments or incrustations around the geysers, hot springs, or steam vents; or to deface the same by written inscription or otherwise; or to throw any substance into the springs or geyser vents; or to injure or disturb in any manner, or to carry off any of the mineral deposits, specimens, natural curiosities, or wonders within the park.
2. It is forbidden to ride or drive upon any of the geyser or hot spring formations or to turn loose stock to graze in their vicinity.
3. It is forbidden to cut or injure any growing timber. Camping parties will be allowed to use dead or fallen timber for fuel.
4. Fires shall be lighted only when necessary, and completely extinguished when not longer required. The utmost care should be exercised at all times to avoid setting fire to the timber and grass, and anyone failing to comply therewith shall be peremptorily removed from the park.
5. Hunting or killing, wounding or capturing, of any bird or wild animal, except dangerous animals, when necessary to prevent them from destroying life or inflicting an injury, is prohibited. The outfits, including guns, traps, teams, horses, or means of transportation used by persons engaged in hunting, killing, trapping, ensnaring, or capturing such birds or wild animals, or in possession of game killed in the park under other circumstances than prescribed above, will be forfeited to the United States, except in cases where it is shown by satisfactory evidence that the outfit is not the property of the person or persons violating this regulation and the actual owner thereof was not a party to such violation. Firearms will only be permitted in the park on written permission from the superintendent thereof. On arrival at the first station of the park guard, parties having firearms will turn them over to the sergeant in charge of the station, taking his receipt for them. They will be returned to the owners on leaving the park.
6. Fishing with nets, seines, traps, or by the use of drugs or explosives, or in any other way than with hook and line, is prohibited. Fishing for purposes of merchandise or profit is forbidden by law. Fishing may be prohibited by order of the superintendent of the park in any of the waters of the park, or limited therein to any specified season of the year, until otherwise ordered by the Secretary of the Interior.
7. No person will be permitted to reside permanently or to engage in any business in the park without permission, in writing, from the Department of the Interior. The superintendent may grant authority to competent persons to act as guides and revoke the same in his discretion, and no pack trains shall be allowed in the park unless in charge of a duly registered guide.
8. The herding or grading of loose stock or cattle of any kind within the park, as well as the driving of such stock or cattle over the roads of the park, is strictly forbidden, except in such cases where authority therefor is granted by the Secretary of the Interior.
9. No drinking saloon or bar room will be permitted within the limits of the park.
10. Private notices or advertisements shall not be posted or displayed within the park, except such as may be necessary for the convenience and guidance of the public, upon buildings on leased ground.
11. Persons who render themselves obnoxious by disorderly conduct or bad behavior, or who violate any of the foregoing rules, will be summarily removed from the park, and will not be allowed to return without permission, in writing, from the Secretary of the Interior or the superintendent of the park.

Any person who violates any of the foregoing regulations will be deemed guilty of a misdemeanor, and be subjected to a fine as provided by the act of Congress approved May 7, 1894, "to protect the birds and animals in Yellowstone National Park and to punish crimes in said park, and for other purposes," of not more than $1,000 or imprisonment not exceeding two years, or both, and be adjudged to pay all costs of the proceedings.

CORNELIUS N. BLISS,
Secretary of the Interior.

INSTRUCTIONS TO PERSONS TRAVELING THROUGH YELLOWSTONE NATIONAL PARK.

DEPARTMENT OF THE INTERIOR,
OFFICE OF SUPERINTENDENT OF YELLOWSTONE NATIONAL PARK,
Mammoth Hot Springs, Wyo., June 20, 1897.

The following instructions, for the information and guidance of parties traveling through the Yellowstone Park, having received the approval of the Secretary of the Interior, are published for the benefit of all concerned.

(1) Fires.—The greatest care must be exercised to insure the complete extinction of all camp fires before they are abandoned. All ashes and unburned bits of wood must, when practicable, be thoroughly soaked with water. Where fires are built in the neighborhood of decayed logs particular attention must be directed to the extinguishment of fires in the decaying mold. Such material frequently smolders for days and then breaks out into dangerous conflagration. Fire may also be extinguished, where water is not available, by a complete covering of earth, well packed down.

(2) Camps.—No camp will be made at a less distance than 100 feet from any traveled road. Blankets, clothing, hammocks, or any other article liable to frighten teams must not be hung at a nearer distance than this to the road. The same rule applies to temporary stops, such as for feeding horses or for taking luncheon.

Camp grounds must be thoroughly cleaned before they are abandoned, and such articles as tin cans, bottles, cast-off clothing, and other débris must be either buried or taken to some place where they will not offend the sight.

(3) Bicycles.—Many of the horses driven in the park are unused to bicycles and liable to be frightened by them. The greatest care must, therefore, be exercised by their riders. In meeting teams, riders will always dismount and stand at the side of the road—the lower side if the meeting be on a grade. In passing teams from the rear, riders will ring their bells as a warning and inquire of the driver if they may pass. If it appear from the answer that the team is liable to be frightened, they may ask the driver to halt his team and allow them to dismount and walk past.

Riders of bicycles are responsible for all damages caused by failure to properly observe these instructions.

(4) Fishing.—All fish less than 6 inches in length should at once be returned to the water with the least damage possible to the fish. No fish should be caught in excess of the number needed for food.

(5) Dogs.—When dogs are taken through the park they must be prevented from chasing the animals and birds or annoying passers-by. To this end they must be carried in the wagons or led behind them while traveling, and kept within the limits of the camps when halted. Any dog found at large in disregard of this section will be killed.

(6) Grazing animals.—Only animals actually in use for purposes of transportation through the park can be grazed in the vicinity of the camps. They will not be allowed to run over any of the formations, nor near to any of the geysers or hot springs; neither will they be allowed to run loose in the roads.

(7) Miscellaneous.—The carving or writing of names or other things on any of the mileposts or signboards, or any of the seats, railings, or other structures, or on the trees, will not be permitted.

Persons are not allowed to bathe near any of the regularly traveled roads in the park without suitable bathing clothes.

(8) Willful disregard of these instructions will result in the ejection of the offending person or persons from the park.

JAMES B. ERWIN,
Captain, Fourth Cavalry,
Acting Superintendent of the Yellowstone National Park.

INSTRUCTIONS FOR STATIONS, MAY, 1898.

OFFICE OF SUPERINTENDENT YELLOWSTONE NATIONAL PARK,
Mammoth Hot Springs, Wyo., May 30, 1898.

GENERAL INSTRUCTIONS.

It is the duty of the stations to see that all the rules and regulations and the instructions to persons traveling through the park are complied with. Parties violating any of these rules or instructions will be promptly placed under arrest and reported to headquarters. If the station is not in telegraphic communication with headquarters the offending persons may be brought in to the nearest telegraph station, where report of the case will be promptly made. Frequent patrols will be made into all the territory belonging to the station for the observation and protection of the game and forests. Particular attention will be paid to the prevention and extinguishing of fires, and when any fire is discovered that can not be controlled by the station an immediate report will be made to headquarters.

When the country is so dry that there is danger of fires along the road, the road will be patrolled every morning.

Each noncommissioned officer will be held responsible for the proper policing of his station and of the ground in its vicinity, and all men on station must, except when scouting, wear the proper uniform and must always be neat and clean. All refuse and slops from camp will be buried.

One man must always be left at the station.

Persons carrying firearms or traps through the park must always have a written permit. This permit must be presented at each station passed and must be carefully scrutinized by the man in charge of the station at the time. If it appears that no undue advantage has been taken of the permit, and if the seals are intact and secure, the permit will be indorsed on the back. If the bearer of the permit appears to have violated the conditions thereof, to have unreasonably delayed between stations, he will be held and the case reported at once to the acting superintendent.

Pack trains entering the park may be given a permit by the noncommissioned officer in charge of a station to come in, traveling by wagon roads only, to the nearest station on their route where there is a commissioned officer. Pack trains will not be allowed off the wagon road without permission in writing from a commissioned officer. Persons in charge of pack trains will be instructed that all vehicles have the right of way over pack trains, and that they will be held responsible for interfering with the progress of wagons or frightening their horses.

All noncommissioned officers in charge of stations will send in to the quartermaster on the 15th and last days of each month all receipts for forage furnished and to their troop commander all receipts for meals.

All stations where a register is kept will forward with their report at the end of each month the number of persons who have been registered during the month. The exterior stations will give the number entering and the number leaving the park by their station. Transcript from register of camping parties will not be sent in.

JAMES B. ERWIN,
Captain, Fourth Cavalry, Acting Superintendent.

SPECIAL INSTRUCTIONS.

Norris.—The territory belonging to this station in summer is that drained by Solfatara Creek, the Gibbon from the head of Virginia meadows to the head of the Gibbon Canyon, Obsidian Creek to the Crystal Springs, and by Straight and Winter creeks.

Road patrols will extend to the Crystal Springs and 5 miles towards the canyon.

This station is charged with the protection of the Norris Basin, and from the time when the first coaches come in until the last one has left one man must remain on the formation. A man must also be on the formation whenever camping parties are there.

The beaver in the neighboring streams must be carefully watched, the same as in winter.

Grand Canyon.—The teritory includes the headwaters of the Gibbon to Virginia Meadows and all the country that drains into the Yellowstone from the Mud Geyser to and including Tower Creek. The beaver in Cascade Creek and lake must be carefully watched. Road patrols will extend 6 miles towards Norris and to the Mud Geyser.

Lake.—The territory includes all the country draining into the Yellowstone River, above Mud Geyser, and all draining into the lake from Beaverdam Creek to Rocky Point. Road patrols will extend from Mud Geyser to 10-mile post towards the Thumb.

All parties passing this station will be registered in the book provided for that purpose.

Upper Basin.—The territory includes all the country that drains into Shoshone Lake from DeLacey Creek to its outlet on the west; all the country that drains into the Firehole River to a point opposite the 5-mile post towards Fountain.

Road patrols will extend 9 miles towards the Thumb and 5 miles towards the Fountain.

A principal and very important duty of this station is to protect the formation from injury or defacement.

50   YELLOWSTONE NATIONAL PARK.

All parties who camp at or in the vicinity of the Upper Basin will be registered in the book provided for that purpose.

Thumb.—The territory includes all the country that drains into the lake from Rock Point to Beaverdam Creek; also the country that drains into Shoshone Lake from DeLacey Creek to its outlet into Lewis River above the falls, and into Heart Lake. While tourists are at the Thumb, one man will be kept on the formation to enforce the regulations.

Road patrols will extend 9 miles towards the Lake Hotel, 10 miles towards the Upper Basin, and to Lewis Falls.

JAMES B. ERWIN,
Captain, Fourth Cavalry, Acting Superintendent.

OFFICE OF SUPERINTENDENT YELLOWSTONE NATIONAL PARK,
Mammoth Hot Springs, Wyo., May 30, 1898.

SPECIAL INSTRUCTIONS.

Parties carrying firearms or traps and desiring to enter the park will be closely questioned as to their intentions and purposes. If they intend to leave the park by the same station by which they entered, they will be required to leave their arms at the station. A receipt will be given, and the arms will be cared for and returned to the owners on their exit from the park.

If the parties desire to pass through the park and leave by some other station, the noncommissioned officer will, if he is satisfied that they are reliable parties, seal their guns and issue a permit on the blank forms provided for that purpose. He will instruct the holder of the permit that he must present it at every station he passes for examination and indorsement, and that any violation of the terms of permit or any undue advantage taken of it will result in his arrest and trial.

When parties leave the park, the permit will be taken up by the last station along the route. It will be properly indorsed and sent to headquarters at the end of the month.

The seals will be removed from the guns when permit is taken up.

JAMES B. ERWIN,
Captain, Fourth Cavalry, Acting Superintendent.

APPENDIX B.

List of parties holding license to conduct camping business.

No.	Name.	Residence.	Number of vehicles.	Duration.
1	G. W. Torbert	Cinnabar, Mont	4	May 26 to Oct. 1, 1898.
2	W. E. Knowles and H. M. Gore.	do	5	May 27 to Oct. 1, 1898.
3	W. S. Dixon	Livingston, Mont	3	May 28 to Oct. 1, 1898.
4	Charlie T. Smith	do	3	Do.
5	Alfred Lycan	Bozeman, Mont	5	Do.
6	W. J. Kupper	Cinnabar, Mont	4	May 30 to Oct. 1, 1898.
7	Adam Gassert	do	5	June 6 to Oct. 1, 1898.
8	S. M. Fitzgerald	Gardiner, Mont	5	Do.
9	B. S. Thresher and O. L. Bishop.	Butte, Mont	5	June 16 to Oct. 1, 1898.
10	A. L. Roseborough	Gardiner, Mont	4	June 27 to Oct. 1, 1898.
11	Marshall Bros	Livingston, Mont	5	June 30 to Oct. 1, 1898.
12	E. V. Blankenship	Bozeman, Mont	5	Do.
13	A. W. Chadbourne	Cinnabar, Mont	5	July 7 to Oct. 1, 1898.
14	Shaw & Powell	Livingston, Mont	4	Aug. 1 to Oct. 1, 1898.
15	A. D. Creasey	Bozeman, Mont	3	Aug. 9 to Oct. 1, 1898.
16	Wm. Wells	Wells P. O., Wyo	2	Sept. 3 to Oct. 1, 1898.
17	G. W. Wakefield	Livingston, Mont	2	Sept. 13 to Oct. 1, 1898

APPENDIX C.

List of registered guides.

No.	Guide.	Residence.	Number of animals.	Duration.
1	William Hague	Fridley, Mont	30	May 31 to Dec. 31, 1898.
2	Richard Randall	Gardiner, Mont	30	July 13 to Dec. 31, 1898.
3	Henry George	Cinnabar, Mont	20	Do.
4	John P. Bean	Bozeman, Mont	20	July 16 to Dec. 31, 1898.
5	James H. Tappan	Dubois, Wyo	20	July 17 to Dec. 31, 1898.
6	Taswell Woody	Pleasant Valley, Y. N. P	30	July 19 to Dec. 31, 1898.
7	Burton Harris	Elk P. O., Wyo	15	July 20 to Dec. 31, 1898.
8	Oliver Paulsell	Red Lodge, Mont	10	July 25 to Aug. 15, 1898.
9	W. T. Hall	Gardiner, Mont	16	July 26 to Dec. 31, 1898.
10	Geo. W. Reese	Cinnabar, Mont	20	Aug. 6 to Dec. 31, 1898.
11	Elwood Hofer	Gardiner, Mont	40	Aug. 10 to Dec. 31, 1898.
12	W. T. Hall	do	40	Do.
13	Frank Randall	do	10	Aug. 22 to Oct. 30, 1898.
14	Geo. Albert Pfohl	Fridley, Mont	16	Aug. 23 to Oct. 31, 1898.
15	O. Paulsell	Red Lodge, Mont	10	Aug. 23 to Sept. 15, 1898.
16	B. D. Sheffield	Livingston, Mont	30	Aug. 23 to Dec. 31, 1898.
17	Frank M. Scott	Gardiner, Mont	15	Aug. 25 to Oct. 31, 1898.
18	Henry Kitchens	Absarokee, Mont	12	Aug. 29 to Oct. 31, 1898.
19	William Nichols	Cooke City, Mont	13	Do.
20	David Black	Chico, Mont	12	Aug. 31 to Nov. 30, 1898.
21	Fountain Black	do	12	Do.
22	Wm. A. Donahoo	Gardiner, Mont	13	Sept. 1 to Oct. 15, 1898.
23	Wm. Wells	Wells P. O., Wyo	20	Sept. 3 to Dec. 31, 1898.

APPENDIX D.

LEASES IN YELLOWSTONE NATIONAL PARK.

Yellowstone Park Transportation Company: Mammoth Hot Springs, 2 acres; Norris, 2 acres; Fountain, 1 acre; Upper Geyser Basin, 2 acres; Lake, 2 acres; Canyon, 1 acre, building, etc., for the accommodation of employees and stock.

Yellowstone Park Association: Mammoth Hot Springs, Mammoth Hotel and commissary; Mammoth Hot Springs, Cottage Hotel and Mammoth Barn; Fountain (Lower Basin), cottages; Fountain, Fountain Hotel and barn; Lake, Lake Hotel and barn; Canyon, Canyon Hotel, pump house, and barn; Upper Geyser Basin, hotel and barn (not yet constructed).

Yellowstone Lake Boat Company: Near Lake Hotel, 2 acres; Frank Island, 2 acres; Stevensons Island, 2 acres; Dot Island, 1 acre; West Thumb, 1 acre; Ways, 2 acres; Southeast Arm, 2 acres; Dot Island Game Corral, 2 acres; to be located by superintendent, 6 acres.

William W. Humphrey and F. Jay Haynes: At Upper Geyser Basin, Thumb, Lake Outlet, Grand Canyon, Norris Geyser Basin, Mammoth Hot Springs, not to exceed 1 acre at each point; building, etc., for the accommodation of employees and stock. (Assignments not yet made.)

Jennie H. Ash: Mammoth Hot Springs, dwelling, post-office, and store.
Ole A. Anderson: Mammoth Hot Springs, dwelling and store.
John F. Yancy: Pleasant Valley, hotel.
F. J. Haynes: Mammoth Hot Springs, studio; Upper Geyser Basin, studio.
Henry E. Klamer: Upper Geyser Basin, dwelling and store.

APPENDIX E.

Statement of cases brought before Hon. John W. Meldrum, United States commissioner, since the 1st day of November, 1897.

January 11.—United States *v.* Thomas J. Miner. Charge: Violation of the provisions of the act of Congress approved May 7, 1894, "to protect the birds and animals in Yellowstone National Park, and to punish crimes in said park, and for other purposes." Trial had February 8. Defendant ordered to pay a fine of $50 and costs.

February 12.—United States *v.* James Herzer. Charge: Violation of the provisions of the act of Congress approved May 7, 1894. Defendant not yet arrested; could not be found within the district of Wyoming.

June 27.—United States *v.* James Courtenay and Richard Murray. Charge: Violation of the provisions of the act of Congress approved May 7, 1894. Separate trial of Richard Murray. Defendant fined $50.

NOTE.—The complaint in this case was filed on the 29th day of October, 1897. Original warrant returned December 18, 1897, "not served." Defendants not found within district of Wyoming. Defendant Murray was brought before the commissioner, by virtue of alias warrant issued June 27. Defendant Courtenay not yet arrested.

July 12.—United States *v.* A. K. Crawford. Charge: Violation of the provisions of the act of Congress approved May 7, 1894. Defendant not yet arrested; could not be found within the district of Wyoming.

August 26.—United States *v.* A. V. Scott. Charge: Violation of the provisions of the act of Congress approved May 7, 1894. Defendant ordered to pay a fine of $25 and costs.

NOTE.—The papers in the cases of United States *v.* James Herzer and A. K. Crawford, respectively, have been transmitted to the United States attorney for the district of Montana, with request that he cause such action to be taken as will place the defendants within the jurisdiction of the authorities of the district of Wyoming.

APPENDIX F.

REPORT OF LIEUTENANT LINDSLEY, FOURTH CAVALRY, ON TRIP TO THE EASTERN FOREST RESERVE.

FORT YELLOWSTONE, WYO., *August 30, 1898.*

SIR: I have the honor to submit the following report of my trip to the eastern forest reserve.

Pursuant to your verbal instructions, I left this post on Sunday the 7th instant with Private Miller, of D Troop. I had ten days' rations, and took two pack mules. Went over the old stage-robber trail. Saw 22 antelope, including 5 kids, on Blacktail Deer Creek; also saw numerous signs of elk and bear. I camped on the extreme head of Lava Creek.

On the 8th I showed Private Miller the cabin on Lava Creek, came by Grebe Lake, then over to Cascade Lake, and down Cascade Creek to the Canyon, then by the wagon road to Mud Geyser. Saw many tracks of elk and deer. The beaver in Cascade Lake and Creek are undisturbed and are doing new work.

On the morning of the 9th Private Rompre, of H Troop, reported to me from the Lake Station and accompanied me. I crossed the river 6 miles from the Lake Hotel, went up Pelican, and by Turbid Lake, and up Bear Creek to the forks, where I camped. Saw 3 elk on the Pelican and plenty of elk and deer signs all the way. Saw a beaver house in Turbid Lake, but had no time to examine it.

On the 10th I crossed the divide by Jones Pass and camped on Jones Creek, under Silver Tip Peak. Private Rompre returned to his station from Bear Creek. Saw 7 elk and plenty of elk and bear signs.

On the morning of the 11th the mules had gone back on the trail, and I sent Miller back after them and remained in camp all day.

On the 12th I rode to the mouth of Jones Creek and examined the trails up and down the North Fork of Stinking Water River. Saw no sign of horses, except the trail of the party which preceded me over Jones Pass a few days before. They had gone down the river. Saw one deer track on the North Fork. Saw where some one had camped last spring at the mouth of Jones Creek and had smoked an elk. On the way back to camp saw where an elk and a lynx had died last spring, probably a natural death, as no parts of the carcass had been removed. Miller returned at 7 p. m. with the mules, which he had found at the lake.

On the 13th I went down to the Stinking Water and followed up it to the mouth of Torrent Creek and camped. Examined the trail to Lamar River. It has not been used recently.

On the 14th I followed the North Fork to its head and crossed the divide to the head of Galena Creek and down it to the head of Sunlight Creek and camped. On the divide I found some shaft timber cut and piled up ready for use. Also found a cabin, not used recently, which I afterwards learned belongs to a Mr. Hughes. On Galena Creek saw a tunnel and a cabin and stable. At the mouth of Galena Creek is another cabin and a fence across the valley. Both sides of the divide are very steep, and a good trail has been built at considerable expense apparently. On the Sunlight side the trail is dug out of slide rock for a large part of the way and it zigzags down the mountain side at a very practicable grade for pack animals. I found a Mr. Campbell and Mr. Vickers camped at the cabin on Sunlight. Last fall

Mr. Campbell located a claim in the gulch between Dyke and Black mountains and built the cabin and fences. He has now brought Mr. Vickers, of Red Lodge, in to inspect the prospect and test the ore, with an idea of building a smelter in case they have sufficient pay ore to warrant it. They had 24 horses, only six of them packed, and intended to stay a month or more.

The old Frenchman of Snake River fame, De Voe, had just come in from Red Lodge and camped near Vickers and Campbell. He had 6 horses (4 packs) loaded with rations, bear traps, etc.; also had 5 stag and bloodhounds. All the men had rifles. De Voe said he had a prospect on Copper Creek and was going to stay in camp a few days and pack some of his ore in for Mr. Vickers to test. Then he wanted to come through the park and go south into Wyoming for the winter. He said he wintered last winter on Wapiti Creek (Elk Fork he calls it), and trapped some bear this spring. I learned next day that he was never known to prospect; that he did winter on Wapiti Creek, and went out about July 1, through Sunlight, with several heads, and went to Red Lodge. Everyone I saw complains of him and his dogs. They say the dogs kill many elk and run the rest out of the country. I was told by Mr. Green, who lives near the junction of the two forks of Stinking Water, that there were dead elk all along the North Fork and its tributaries, killed last winter by De Voe's dogs.

On the 15th I went down Sunlight to the "Basin" and camped at Tighe's ranch. Remained there on the 16th and saw every ranch and nearly every settler in the reserve. Learned that Mr. Webster, for whom I was looking, has not come in that way.

On the 17th I went on down Sunlight to Dead Indian Creek and up it to near its head.

On the 18th I went down Rattlesnake to the North Fork and camped at Mr. Green's ranch.

On the 19th I crossed over to the South Fork and came up it by Marquette and Ishawood post-offices and camped at Col. W. F. Cody's ranch, at the mouth of Ishawood and close to the Forest Reserve line. At Mr. Green's I learned that no party had gone up the North Fork this year and only the party from the park had come down.

On the 20th I went up the South Fork to Captain Darley's ranch, making the acquaintance of all the settlers on the way.

On the 21st I went on up as far as McLaughlin's ranch (Valley Home). This is the farthest settler up the South Fork except Mr. Davis, whom I met at Captain Darley's. I then returned to Cody's ranch and camped.

On the 22d I came up Ishawood to near its head.

On the 23d I crossed the Ishawood Pass and came down Pass Creek to the Thorofare and down it to the Yellowstone.

On the 24th I came to the mouth of the Upper Yellowstone and camped, and on the 25th came to the Lake Hotel and camped near the station, ferrying my stuff over the river and swimming my stock.

On the 26th I laid over to let my stock rest, and went to the Thumb by boat for my mail. Found the station there in excellent condition as to police and neatness. On returning to Lake, I saw a big volume of smoke rising from behind Flat Mountain, which I reported to the superintendent by wire. In obedience to your telegraphic orders to locate the fire and find out its size, I then went in the Government boat, with Sergeant Welch and Private Montgomery and Mr. Bowers, to the south arm of the lake. We ran on a bar at Frank Island and had to go ashore in a rowboat, which I had procured from Mr. Waters, and cut some big levers; then got out, waded on the bar, and pried her off. When we reached the south arm it was too dark to go further, so we camped.

The 27th I climbed on foot to the top of the divide, but could not satisfactorily locate the fire from there, so I put the boat into the Flat Mountain arm, made a landing and we climbed Flat Mountain, but had to go on to within 2 miles of Heart Lake before we could locate the fire, on the point between Barlows Fork and Heart River. It rained very hard in the morning, and when I saw the fire it was smoking but evidently not burning very hard. It was over a mile long, however. We returned to the boat and then to the hotel. It rained very hard this evening.

On the 28th I came from the lake to the Canyon, and on the 29th reached this post, having been out twenty-two days, on ten days' rations, plus what I had bought en route.

I saw several elk tracks on Ishawood, perhaps half a dozen, and on Thorofare and the Yellowstone River and Lake saw plenty of elk signs. Saw several moose tracks along the Upper Yellowstone, Thorofare, and the Lake. The beaver dams in Thorofare are deserted, as they are in Beaverdam and Trappers Creek, and all the creeks. There are some bank beaver in the Yellowstone which have escaped the trappers who despoil the colonies in the smaller streams. This is an ideal moose, elk, and beaver colony, and if a station were put at the mouth of Thorofare, and that country protected, all the streams would soon fill up with beaver, and the moose would increase.

The necessity for a station there and one on Falls River has long been recognized, and now, with the increase in the troops, it will perhaps be practicable.

I saw no game whatever in the reserve, and, except one deer track and a few elk, saw no game signs except in the Thorofare country.

Following is a list of settlers in Sunlight Basin, within the forest reserve:

Gust Lafond, single, claimed a ranch last fall. There was a cabin on the place; has made no improvements and does not live on his claim; has 6 or 8 head of cattle.

Mrs. Chatfield. Mr. Chatfield located on Sunlight previous to 1891. He died last winter and his widow occupies the place. She has 33 head of cattle and a few horses; has a fair cabin, corrals, and stable, and has a meadow under fence and ditch. Mr. Chatfield also had a number of mining claims in the reserve.

Charles Hoff located previous to 1891; has 9 head of cattle and 20 horses; has comfortable cabin and good corrals and stable; has a meadow under fence and ditch; has no mining claims.

John Hughes has been in the country a long time and has several mines up the creek. Took up a ranch and built a house last winter. Has no cattle; about 25 work horses.

Jack Tighe located his ranch in April, 1891, and left for the winter, coming back in 1892, since when he has resided permanently on his place. Tighe has about 6 head of cattle and a few horses; has a pasture under fence and will turn it into a meadow as soon as he completes his ditch. Has a comfortable cabin and fair sheds and corrals. Is married. Cuts no hay. Works for other people some, in mines.

Williard Ruscher took up claim last year. Has cabin; poor fences; no stock; cuts no hay. Works in mines and on ranches.

Henry Delaney built cabin last winter; single; has no stock and no fence; works for other people.

John R. Painter has family. Came from Philadelphia three years ago. Located last summer close to line of forest reserve. Has two good cabins and good stable. Has nearly completed a good house of peeled logs, two stories, five rooms on ground floor, shingle roof, large windows, matched floor, etc. Has three miles or more of good wire fence around field which he uses now as a pasture. Intends to get water on it next year and then cut hay on it. Has several cattle, horses, and mules. Came here to engage in mining. Mr. Painter has purchased the interests of Messrs. Malin and Pratt, Baronette and Miller, also part of the interests of Mr. Hughes, and has an entire or a controlling interest in some half dozen mines—the Silver Tip, Evening Star, Rainbow, Pilgrim, Novelty, and others. He has expended considerable money in building roads and trails and developing his mines. He told me he has invested about $25,000 in the forest reserve. He has shipped about 27 tons of ore, which averaged at the smelter $152 per ton, and is now getting out six cars of ore to ship to Omaha. This ore he packs on mules about 10 or 12 miles to the mouth of Sulphur Creek, then hauls 55 miles in wagons to Red Lodge, whence it goes over the Northern Pacific Railroad to Billings and down the Burlington to Omaha. The cost of working, transporting, and mining the ore he reports to be about $50, leaving him $100 per ton profit. He is working several men in the Evening Star at present, besides the men engaged in transporting the ore to the railroad. He intends to put in a stamp mill and concentrator on the Silver Tip property next year.

Following is a list of settlers on Shoshone River, and within the reserve:

A. E. Swanson settled in 1895; fair log house and stable; 3 miles of fence; 1¼ miles of ditch; 12 acres hay; 15 in wheat and oats; 4 head of cattle, 20 horses.

W. H. Jordan settled in 1897; has fair log cabin and stable; 2 miles wood fence; 2 miles ditch; cuts 30 tons of hay; 7 acres in grain; 36 cattle and 7 horses.

John Davis settled in May, 1891; log house and 2 stables; 1¼ mile fence; ¼ mile ditch; cuts 15 tons hay; 7¼ acres grain; 7 cattle, 8 horses; is a Welchman and miner.

Duff Putnam settled in 1896; 1-room cabin; 2 stables; 160 acres under fence; 300 yards ditch; cuts 10 tons hay; 12 head cattle, 4 horses.

Capt. Henry A. C. Darley is an ex-officer of Royal Artillery; bachelor; settled in 1897; has fair 3-room house and fair stable; 1 mile wire fence, 1¼ miles wood fence; 1½ miles ditch; cuts 50 tons hay; has small field oats this year; 80 cattle and 30 horses; hunts for sport only; has 2 mining claims.

Mrs. E. C. Brown settled April 21, 1894; has fair cabin, several rooms; old, fair stable; 2 miles wood fence; 1 mile ditch; cuts 30 tons hay; has a little barley; 24 cattle, about 100 horses; her son, Nona Brown, is a professional guide, but disclaims to be a hunter, and his neighbors say he is not a hunter.

E. M. Brown settled April 21, 1894; has fair cabin and stable; 2 miles wood fence; 1 mile ditch; cuts 30 tons hay; has no cattle; 4 horses.

James McLaughlin settled in 1889 or 1890; has 3 good cabins, a stable; about 1 mile good fence; 1½ miles ditch; cuts 40 tons hay, and has a fine vegetable garden; 30 head cattle, 9 horses; is a hunter and trapper, but of late devotes his time to ranching and sometimes guides parties to the park; bears a fine reputation among all his neighbors as being absolutely reliable and honest, intelligent, and industrious.

John Hurst; single; settled in 1894; has a good cabin and corral; no stable; 1½ miles wire fence; ¼ mile ditch; cuts 10 tons hay, and has 8 horses; bears a good reputation; Captain Darley gives him a high recommendation as a guide and hunter; is a young man, and seems honest and very intelligent.

Many of these ranches, both on South Fork and on Sunlight, were located and occupied previous to the dates given above, upon which they were first occupied by their present occupants. These two valleys are the only parts of the reserve which are suitable for agriculture or stock raising. In both places stock winters with very little feed and the snow fall is light.

In view of the improvements put there in good faith by settlers, it seems best to me to allow these valleys to be used, as they are of no use as a reserve.

In the Shoshone mining region many claims have been located and represented, some for several years, but no real development work has been done on any of them. In the Sunlight district considerable development has been done, and I would recommend that suitable regulations be promulgated, allowing settlers to use any suitable lands for agricultural and stock-raising purposes, allowing prospecting and mining operations to be carried on, and the necessary amount of timber to be used, under wise regulations which would prevent waste or spoliation of the forests; that the reservation be not added to the park, except such part of it in the south as drains into the Yellowstone River; that the game laws of Wyoming be enforced in the reserve; and that either a detail of soldiers be made to enforce these regulations or that the reserve be placed under charge of proper civil officials for its administration and protection.

Very respectfully,
ELMER LINDSLEY,
First Lieutenant, First Cavalry.

The ACTING SUPERINTENDENT YELLOWSTONE NATIONAL PARK,
Present.

APPENDIX G.

SCHEDULE MONIDA AND YELLOWSTONE STAGE COMPANY.

Both ways via Monida:
First day.—Leave Monida 8.30 a. m., arrive Shambow 12.30 p. m.; leave Shambow 1.30 p. m., arrive Dwelle's 5.30 p. m.
Second day.—Leave Dwelle's 8 a. m., arrive Fountain Hotel 11.30 a. m.
Third day.—Leave Fountain Hotel 8 a. m., arrive Upper Basin 10 a. m.; leave Upper Basin 4.30 p. m., arrive Fountain Hotel 6 p. m.
Fourth day.—Leave Fountain Hotel 7.30 a. m., arrive West Bay 1 p. m.; leave West Bay 3 p. m., arrive Lake Hotel 5 p. m.
Fifth day.—Leave Lake Hotel 9 a. m., arrive Canyon Hotel 12 noon.
Sixth day.—Leave Canyon Hotel 9.30 a. m., arrive Norris 12 noon; leave Norris 1.30 p. m., arrive Mammoth Springs 4 p. m.
Seventh day.—Leave Mammoth Springs 8 a. m., arrive Norris 12 noon; leave Norris 1.30 p. m., arrive Dwelle's 5.30 p. m.
Eighth day.—Leave Dwelle's 8 a. m., arrive Shambow 12 noon; leave Shambow 1 p. m., arrive Monida 6 p. m.

In Monida and out via Cinnabar:
First day.—Leave Monida 8.30 a. m., arrive Shambow 12.30 p. m.; leave Shambow 1.30 p. m., arrive Dwelle's 5.30 p. m.
Second day.—Leave Dwelle's 8 a. m., arrive Fountain Hotel 11.30 a. m.
Third day.—Leave Fountain Hotel 8 a. m., arrive Upper Basin 10 a. m.; leave Upper Basin 4.30 p. m., arrive Fountain Hotel 6 p. m.
Fourth day.—Leave Fountain Hotel 7.30 a. m., arrive West Bay 1 p. m.; leave West Bay 3 p. m., arrive Lake Hotel 5 p. m.
Fifth day.—Leave Lake Hotel 9 a. m., arrive Canyon Hotel 12 noon.
Sixth day.—Leave Canyon Hotel 9 30 a. m., arrive Norris 12 noon; leave Norris 1.30 p. m., arrive Mammoth Springs 4 p. m.; leave Mammoth Springs 6.30 p. m., arrive Cinnabar 8 p. m.

Direct connections made at Cinnabar with Northern Pacific Railroad for St. Paul.

56 YELLOWSTONE NATIONAL PARK.

METEOROLOGICAL REGISTER, FORT YELLOWSTONE, WYO.

SEPTEMBER, 1897.

Date.	Maximum.	Minimum.	Range	Winds.	Precipitation	Remarks.
1	75	42	33	SW.		
2	81	42	39	S.		
3	59	52	7	NW.		
4	64	44	20	SW.		
5	77	49	28	S.		
6	77	45	32	SW.	Trace	
7	79	58	21	S.		
8	55	47	8	NW.		
9	53	26	27	S.		
10	55	33	22	S.		
11	71	39	32	NW.	Trace	
12	66	36	30	S.	Trace	
13	75	37	38	S.	Trace	
14	56	41	15	S.		
15	51	41	10	NW.		
16	61	28	33	S.		
17	74	33	41	S.		
18	72	35	37	NW.		
19	75	35	40	S.		
20	74	37	37	S.		
21	78	37	41	S.		
22	74	42	32	NW.		
23	70	45	25	SW.		
24	73	37	36	S.		
25	76	37	39	S.		
26	70	41	35	S.		
27	73	46	27	S.		
28	66	43	23	SW.	0.27	Rain.
29	67	38	29	S.		
30	72	42	30	SW.	.04	Rain.
Total	2,091	1,218	873		.31	
Mean	69.70	40.60	29.10	S.		

Maximum, 81° on 2d instant; minimum, 26° on 9th instant; mean, 55.15°; total precipitation, 0.31 inch; prevailing winds, south.

OCTOBER, 1897.

Date.	Maximum.	Minimum.	Range	Winds.	Precipitation	Remarks.
1	56	40	16	SW.	0.27	Rain and sleet.
2	48	37	11	S.	.16	Snow (first storm season).
3	56	30	26	SW.		
4	62	34	28	SW.		
5	68	34	34	W.	.09	Rain.
6	72	35	37	SW.		
7	64	49	15	NW.		
8	54	34	20	S.		
9	58	33	25	NW.		
10	56	28	28	SW.		
11	55	41	14	NW.	.08	Rain.
12	54	35	19	N.	.67	Snow.
13	38	27	11	N.	.15	Snow.
14	32	23	9	N.		
15	13	9	14	W.		
16	38	14	24	N.		
17	44	20	24	W.		
18	48	24	24	S.		
19	58	26	32	S.	.04	Rain.
20	54	31	23	S.	.08	Rain.
21	63	33	30	SW.		
22	44	40	4	N.		
23	48	36	12	N.	.20	Snow.
24	50	38	12	N.		
25	38	30	8	NW.		
26	33	29	4	W.		
27	41	16	25	S.		
28	55	26	29	S.		
29	59	29	30	SW.		
30	52	30	22	SW.		
31	55	26	29	SW.		
Total	1,586	950	636		1.72	
Mean	51.16	30.64	20.51	SW.		

Maximum, 72° on 6th instant; minimum, 14° on 16th instant; mean, 40.90°; total precipitation, 1.72 inches; prevailing winds, southwest.

NOVEMBER, 1897.

Date.	Maximum.	Minimum.	Range	Winds.	Precipitation	Remarks.
1	39	29	10	S.		
2	59	30	29	S.		
3	56	31	25	N.	0.38	Snow. Earthquake at 2.30 a.m.
4	39	37	2	N.		
5	34	14	20	W.	.20	Snow.
6	33	22	11	S.	.10	Snow.
7	31	15	16	N.	.15	Snow.
8	25	11	14	W.		
9	27	7	20	S.		
10	42	18	24	S.		
11	44	30	14	S.	.19	Rain.
12	47	34	13	S.	.11	Rain.
13	52	43	9	W.	.30	Snow.
14	48	35	13	N.		
15	28	20	8	NW.		
16	22	9	13	SW.		
17	34	10	24	S.		
18	49	30	19	S.		
19	47	38	9	S.		
20	54	40	14	W.	.55	Snow.
21	40	16	24	NW.	.40	Snow.
22	33	6	27	SW.		
23	37	21	16	N.		
24	45	33	12	N.		
25	38	23	15	NW.	.05	Snow.
26	31	13	18	S.		
27	26	21	5	N.	.30	Snow.
28	24	6	18	S.	.15	Snow.
29	26	1	25	S.	.10	Snow.
30	35	21	14	S.		
Total	1,145	664	481		2.98	
Mean	38.16	22.13	16.03	S.		

Maximum, 59° on 2d instant; minimum, 1° on 29th instant; mean, 30.15°; total precipitation, 2.98 inches; prevailing winds, south.

METEOROLOGICAL REGISTER, FORT YELLOWSTONE, WYO.—Continued.

DECEMBER, 1897.

Date.	Maximum.	Minimum.	Range.	Winds.	Precipitation.	Remarks.
1	30	15	15	S.		
2	28	7	21	S.		
3	23	—5	28	N.		
4	29	11	18	SW.	0.05	Snow.
5	30	19	11	W.		
6	37	23	14	SW.		
7	35	29	6	S.	.10	Snow.
8	36	25	11	S.	.45	Snow.
9	27	19	8	S.		
10	31	19	12	SW.		
11	31	18	13	S.		
12	32	23	9	S.	.10	Snow.
13	33	14	19	N.		
14	30	16	14	N.		
15	0	—5	5	S.		
16	6	—19	25	SW.		
17	16	3	20	S.		
18	17	3	14	S.		
19	18	1	12	NE.		
20	13	3	10	S.		
21	16	7	18	S.		
22	25	5	24	S.		
23	29	19	8	S.		
24	27	15	12	S.		
25	29	13	16	S.		
26	31	25	9	S.		
27	34	30	7	N.		
28	37	15	8	SW.	.10	Snow.
29	37	—6	21	NW.		
30	23	15		S.		
31	15	—6				
Total	807	374	433		.80	
Mean	26.03	12.06	13.96			

Maximum, 37° on 6th, 28th, and 29th instant; minimum, —19° on 16th instant; mean, 19.04°; total precipitation, 0.80 inch; prevailing winds, south.

JANUARY, 1898.

Date.	Maximum.	Minimum.	Range.	Winds.	Precipitation.	Remarks.
1	25	3	22	S.		
2	39	9	30	NW.		
3	36	25	11	S.		
4	37	15	12	SW.		
5	32	25	7	SW.		
6	34	25	9	S.		
7	32	20	12	S.		Snow.
8	23	15	8	SW.	0.01	Snow.
9	23	13	10	NW.	.10	Snow.
10	17	1	16	SW.	.20	
11	15	—3	12	S.		
12	16	6	10	N.	Trace	
13	18	4	14	NW.		
14	25	—10	21	N.		
15	22	12	15	SE.		
16	21	4	10	SW.		
17	27	5	17	SW.		
18	23	15	19	S.		
19	20	5	12	N.		
20	17	3	18	N.		
21	18	8	23	N.		
22	10	—8	9	NW.		
23	8	—20	19	N.		
24	9	—15	30	SW.		
25	9	—6	23	N.		
26	19	1	15	NW.		
27	23	6	16	SW.		
28	26	13	29	N.		
29	30	13	21	S.		
30	33	—6	17	SW.	.31	
31			24			
Total	717	310	511			
Mean	23.12	10.00	16.48			

Maximum, 39° on 2d instant; minimum, —20° on 24th instant; mean, 14.72°; total precipitation, 0.31 inch; prevailing winds, southwest.

FEBRUARY, 1898.

Date.	Maximum.	Minimum.	Range.	Winds.	Precipitation.	Remarks.
1	32	10	22	S.		
2	31	5	26	S.		
3	31	18	13	SW.		
4	30	19	11	S.	0.01	Snow.
5	39	19	20	S.	Trace	
6	38	32	6	SW.		
7	37	31	5	SW.		
8	40	22	9	N.		
9	39	22	17	S.		
10	26	7	19	S.		
11	34	12	22	S.		
12	34	13	21	SW.		
13	36	23	12	S.		
14	33	21	12	S.		
15	41	29	12	SW.		
16	38	33	5	NW.	.10	Snow.
17	37	16	21	N.	.80	Snow.
18	13	1	12	N.	.10	Snow.
19	20	3	17	S.		
20	29	8	21	S.		
21	36	19	19	NW.		
22	39	20	19	N.	.20	Snow.
23	28	5	23	NW.		
24	39	2	30	SW.		
25	32	9	36	N.		
26	45	21	14	SW.		
27	35	13	26	S.		
28	39	12	33	S.		
	45	23	19		1.21	
Total	963	446	517			
Mean	34.39	15.92	18.46			

Maximum, 45° on 24th and 27th instant; minimum, 1° on 17th instant; mean, 25.15°; total precipitation, 1.21 inches; prevailing winds, south.

METEOROLOGICAL REGISTER, FORT YELLOWSTONE, WYO.—Continued.

MARCH, 1898.

Date.	Maximum.	Minimum.	Range.	Winds.	Precipitation.	Remarks.
1	40	26	14	N.		
2	44	24	20	S.		
3	39	27	12	SW.		
4	37	25	12	NW.		
5	41	17	24	S.		
6	43	20	23	SW.		
7	45	23	22	SE.	0.20	Snow.
8	40	18	22	NW.		
9	23	17	6	N.		
10	24	2	23	N.		
11	26	−1	25	NW.	.10	
12	32	2	30	SW.	Trace	
13	32	19	13	NW.	.30	Snow.
14	27	13	14	NW.		
15	29	7	22	N.		
16	24	0	24	N.		
17	32	−2	34	N.	Trace	
18	26	7	19	NW.	Trace	
19	25	6	19	NW.	.30	Snow.
20	30	−4	11	S.	.50	Snow.
21	26	−22	30	NW.		
22	18	6	19	S.		
23	25	18	17	NW.		
24	35	28	14	NW.		
25	32	8	16	N.		
26	21	−1	30	NW.		
27	25	6	33	SW.		
28	29	1	30	SW.		
29	29	−13	19	SW.		
30	32	13	21	SW.		
31	34	13				
Total	964	326	638		1.40	
Mean	31.09	10.51	20.58	NW.		

Maximum, 45° on 7th instant; minimum, −22° on 22d instant; mean, 20.80°; total precipitation, 1.40 inches; prevailing winds, northwest.

APRIL, 1898.

Date.	Maximum.	Minimum.	Range.	Winds.	Precipitation.	Remarks.
1	44	6	38	SW.		
2	51	27	24	SW.		
3	31	24	7	NW.		
4	38	18	20	S.	0.10	Snow.
5	46	12	34	SW.		
6	50	22	28	SW.	.05	Snow.
7	38	25	13	S.		
8	38	25	17	SW.		
9	42	31	21	SW.		
10	54	32	27	SW.	.30	Snow.
11	59	31	20	SW.		
12	51	25	25	SW.		
13	54	30	30	SW.		
14	59	34	34	NE.		
15	65	22	22	NE.		
16	68	36	12	NE.		
17	58	35	20	NE.		
18	47	28	28	N.		
19	48	24	22	NE.	.30	Snow.
20	52	31	17	NW.		
21	53	37	17	SE.		
22	54	35	22	SW.		
23	51	32	17	NE.		
24	62	28	34	NW.		
25	67	34	33	NW.		
26	68	43	25	W.		
27	52	39	32	SW.		
28	59	27	32	NW.		
29	55	30	25	SW.	.20	Snow.
30	42	28	14	NW.		
Total	1,573	859	714		.95	
Mean	52.43	28.63	23.80	SW.		

Maximum, 68° on 15th and 26th instant; minimum, 6° on 1st instant; mean, 41.03°; total precipitation, 0.95 inch; prevailing winds, southwest.

MAY, 1898.

Date.	Maximum.	Minimum.	Range.	Winds.	Precipitation.	Remarks.
1	38	26	12	NW.	Trace	
2	35	24	11	N.	Trace	
3	40	25	15	N.		
4	44	25	19	NW.	Trace	
5	54	23	31	SW.	Trace	
6	59	30	29	W.		
7	54	39	15	NW.		
8	59	30	29	W.		
9	65	30	35	W.		
10	70	35	35	SW.		
11	62	43	19	W.		
12	58	37	21	SW.		
13	65	35	30	NW.	0.15	Rain.
14	65	34	31	NW.		
15	61	34	27	N.		
16	56	37	19	N.	.30	Rain.
17	51	40	11	SE.	.15	Rain.
18	54	37	17	SW.	.10	Snow.
19	52	35	15	NW.		
20	47	30	17	SW.		
21	58	32	26	NW.		
22	62	40	22	NW.	0.45	Rain.
23	58	40	18	N.		
24	48	37	11	NE.		
25	55	40	15	NE.		
26	59	42	17	SW.		
27	73	39	34	NW.		Rain.
28	58	41	17	SW.	.45	Rain.
29	58	36	22	SW.	.10	Rain.
30	56	38	18	SW.	.25	Rain and sleet.
31	52	29	23	SW.		
Total	1,726	1,065	661		1.95	
Mean	55.67	34.35	21.32	SW.		

Maximum, 73° on 27th instant; minimum, 23° on 5th instant; mean, 47.51°; total precipitation, 1.95 inches; prevailing winds, southwest.

METEOROLOGICAL REGISTER, FORT YELLOWSTONE, FORT YELLOWSTONE, WYO.—Continued.

JUNE, 1898.

Date.	Maximum.	Minimum.	Range.	Winds.	Precipitation.	Remarks.
1	61	39	22	SW.	0.32	Rain.
2	53	35	18	NW.		
3	46	31	15	NW.	.15	Rain.
4	48	36	12	NW.		
5	52	34	18	NW.	.02	Rain.
6	56	34	22	NW.		
7	64	31	33	NW.		
8	65	32	32	NW.		
9	69	35	34	NW.		
10	(a)	38		W.	.50	Rain.
11	(a)	40		NW.		
12	(a)	43		NW.	.20	Rain.
13	(a)	45		W.	.15	Rain.
14	(a)	39		SW.		
15	(a)	52		S.		
16	(a)	49		S.		
17	80	55	31	S.		
18	87	49	38	SE.		
19	87	55	32	S.		
20	76	39	37	S.	.33	Rain.
21	74	38	35	NW.	.45	Rain.
22	83	18	18	S.		
23	71	20	20	SW.		
24	66	36	36	S.		
25	68	30	30	SW.		
26	71	35	36	NW.	.38	Rain.
27	80	46	34	NW.	.15	n.
28	76	46	30	N.		
29	73	34	39			
30	70	42	28			
Total		1,252			2.67	
Mean		41.70		NW.		

Maximum, not known; minimum, 31° on 3d instant; mean, not known; total precipitation, 2.67 inches; prevailing winds, northwest.

JULY, 1898.

Date.	Maximum.	Minimum.	Range.	Winds.	Precipitation.	Remarks.
1	50	39	11	N.		
2	67	32	35	W.		
3	76	40	36	SW.		
4	80	47	33	SW.		
5	81	53	28	SW.	0.15	Rain.
6	78	44	34	SW.	.20	Rain.
7	81	49	32	SW.		
8	80	47	33	SW.		
9	79	45	34	SW.		Rain.
10	86	51	35	S.		
11	87	49	38	SW.		
12	77	57	20	S.	.60	
13	79	49	30	SW.		
14	86	52	34	W.		
15	86	52	34	SW.		
16	77	51	35	SW.		
17	66	48	29	SW.		
18	70	39	27	W.		
19	80	43	27	SW.		
20	77	39	41	SW.	.10	Rain.
21	72	52	25	SW.		
22	81	47	36	SW.		
23	87	40	41	S.		
24	87	46	41	SW.		
25	82	49	33	W.		
26	83	47	36	N.		
27	81	45	36	NW.		
28	81	58	35	N.		
29	72	46	27	NW.		
30	76	45	39	N.		
31					1.15	
Total	2,425	1,427	998			
Mean	78.23	46.03	32.20	SW.		

Maximum, 87° on 11th and 25th instant; minimum, 32° on 2d instant; mean, 62.13°; total precipitation, 1.15 inches; prevailing winds, southwest.

AUGUST, 1898.

Date.	Maximum.	Minimum.	Range.	Winds.	Precipitation.	Remarks.
1	73	48	25	N.		Rain.
2	78	40	38	N.		
3	84	47	37	N.		
4	81	47	34	N.		
5	67	49	18	N.	0.10	
6	74	37	37	NW.		
7	79	42	37	N.		
8	84	46	38	E.		
9	85	49	36	SW.		
10	84	54	30	SW.		
11	84	50	34	SW.		
12	89	54	35	W.		
13	74	50	24	SW.		
14	70	50	20	W.	.25	
15	76	53	23	W.	.30	
16	76	49	27	SW.	.15	
17	72	44	34	SW.		
18	78	42	42	SW.		
19	84	42	42	NW.		
20	86	49	38	SW.		
21	87	55	28	SW.		
22	83	44	37	NW.		
23	74	40	43	SW.		Rain.
24	77	41	41	SW.	.50	
25	84	42	43	NW.		
26	83	45	41	SW.		
27	85	58	27	SW.		
28	80	48	34	NW.	.15	Rain.
29	76	45	31	SW.	.45	Rain.
30	68	50	18	SW.	.15	Rain.
31	68	43	25			
Total	2,455	1,451	1,004		2.05	
Mean	79.19	46.81	32.39	SW.		

Maximum, 89° on 12th instant; minimum, 37° on 6th instant; mean, 63°; total precipitation, 2.05 inches; prevailing winds, southwest.

a Thermometer broken.

Diary of Yellowstone Park scouts, winter season of 1897-98.

[George Whittaker, 1897.]

November 6.—Left Mammoth Hot Springs for Norris; arrived at Norris 7.30 p. m. Saw 5 elk on Swan Lake Meadow, 2 coyotes at Willow Park. Weather cloudy and cold.

November 7.—Left Norris station at 9.30 a. m., and proceeded to Mud Geyser; arrived Mud Geyser 6 p. m. Saw 25 elk 1 mile west of Canyon Junction, large band near Sulphur Mountain, 172 on east side of Yellowstone River, opposite mouth of Alum Creek; 1 red fox and 3 coyotes at Trout Creek bridge. Weather very cold and snowing heavy.

November 8.—Left Mud Geyser station and crossed Yellowstone River in a boat. Went on foot for about 4 miles east, making about 8 miles in all. Saw 1 deer track, 2 red foxes. Weather storming and cold.

November 9.—Left Mud Geyser station with Sergeant Simons and Private Akers and proceeded to Pelican Creek cabin. Saw 1 elk. Weather, blinding snowstorm all day.

November 10.—Left cabin with Sergeant Simons, dismounted, for Pelican Cone and Mush Kettles on Pelican Creek; made a circuit of about 10 miles; almost impossible to travel with horses. Weather stormy. Saw 1 elk.

November 11.—Left cabin with Sergeant Simons, mounted, for head of Astringent Creek and White Lake. Left Private Akers at cabin until we returned. Proceeded about 4 miles on horses, then proceeded on foot to south end of White Lake; could not get there with horses on account of deep snow. Saw no sign of any kind all day. Snow between 2 and 3 feet deep on the head of Astringent Creek. Weather stormy.

November 12.—Left cabin for head of Raven Creek, mounted; proceeded as far as beaver dams, where snow was too deep to travel with horses. Saw some fresh beaver sign. Decided to go back to Mud Geyser station for grain and rations and return in three or four days. No sign of any other game. Weather, snowing and raining; snow going very fast.

November 13.—Left Mud Geyser station for Trout Creek cabin, with snowshoe rations for cabin; took Sergeant Simons and Private Akers to assist me in putting wood in cabin, and show them route to Thumb in winter time. Saw no sign of game in Hayden Valley, something very unusual at this time of the year. Weather cold and stormy.

November 14.—Left Trout Creek cabin for Fountain station; decided to take Sergeant Simons and Private Akers with me and return to Mud Geyser from Fountain and go back to Pelican as soon as I get through at this place. Had intended to go up to Bear Parks and Shoshone Geyser Basin and take Corporal Holman and one private with me, but corporal informed me that he had just returned from Bear Parks five days ago and saw no sign of any game in there, and had also tried to get to Shoshone Geyser Basin with horses, and the deep snow drove him back. There being nothing further to detain me here, I decided to return to Mud Geyser to-morrow and try the Pelican Creek again. Left Trout Creek cabin at 11.45 a. m. and got to foot of Mary's Mountain about 1 p. m. After we got to Snow cabin at foot of mountain I saw two very fresh tracks, should say half hour old; examined them closely and saw they were buffalo; about half mile farther came onto two more tracks, which proved to be buffalo also, but not so large as first two, and one more half mile east of Magpie Creek; thought best not to pursue them; presume they were somewhere back of Fountain Hotel all summer and are just moving into Hayden Valley. Some beaver sign in Nez Perce Creek. Weather very cold and stormy.

November 15.—The stock being very tired, and it being very cold and stormy, I decided to lay over to-day and return to Mud Geyser to-morrow; and by the time I got a telephone message in to post about buffalo it was 11 a. m. before I got back to station, almost too late to start for Mud Geyser. Requested Corporal Holman to ride up to Twin Buttes and see if there were any buffalo sign there. He returned and reported nothing but elk sign and some beaver sign in Sentinel Creek. Weather cold and stormy.

November 16.—Left station for Mud Geyser station with Sergeant Simons and Private Akers via Marys Mountain. Arrived at station 4.30 p. m. Saw 15 elk on Nez Perce Creek at foot of Mary's Mountain. Observed that Corporal Holman is very attentive to the duty assigned him to prevent poaching in the park. Weather cloudy and cold.

November 17.—Stayed at Mud Geyser station to start for Pelican Creek to-morrow; there being some work to do pertaining to my stock and saddles, was too late to make a start to-day. Weather clear and cold.

November 18.—Left Mud Geyser station with Sergeant Simons and Private Murphy for Pelican Creek cabin, intending to go up to Mirror Plateau and head of Flint Creek. Arrived at cabin at 4 p. m. Saw 14 swan on Yellowstone River above ford. Weather cloudy.

November 19.—Left cabin for Mirror Plateau, but found, after proceeding about 5 miles, the snow so deep and hard that could not go there, so tried to go up to summit of the mountain and go down Willow Creek, but could not get there, so had to turn back. Could do nothing with horses on account of snow. Saw two buffalo tracks on Astringent Creek; quite a number of elk sign on Pelican Creek. Weather cold and stormy.

November 20.—Left cabin for Mud Geyser station with intention of returning to post, it being useless to try to do anything with horses. Saw 27 swan on river above ford. Weather stormy and cold.

November 21.—Left Mud Geyser for Norris; arrived at Norris at 5.30 p. m. In my experience with the detachment at Mud Geyser I found that they were preventing any poaching being done in their district. A band of about 200 elk crossed the river above Alum Creek, just as I came by. Weather cloudy and cold.

November 22.—Left Norris station for Fort Yellowstone; stayed back with teamster to remove large rock out of road, but could not remove it; tried to pull it out, but could not. Fixed telephone wire at Crystal Spring. Saw a band of about 200 elk at Swan Lake; about 75 elk in the timber about 1 mile post from post; 15 deer at Golden Gate. Weather cloudy.

[James G. Morrison, 1897.]

November 24.—Left the post with Privates McReynolds and Miller to go over on the Gallatin. On account of the deep snow we got no farther than the pocket on Fawn Creek, where we camped. Saw about 750 elk; also numerous signs of beaver on the Gardiner River and Fawn Creek. Distance traveled, about 12 miles.

November 25.—Took back trail down Fawn Creek about 4 miles, thence south along Quadrant Mountain to Indian Creek and up it about 4 miles to snowshoe shack, where we camped. Saw about 150 elk; many signs of beaver on this creek. Distance traveled, about 15 miles.

November 26.—Remained in camp, scouting up Indian Creek. No signs of game. Distance traveled, about 10 miles.

November 27.—Proceeded to the post. Distance, 12 miles.

[George Whittaker, 1897.]

November 23 to 25.—Doing duty at Fort Yellowstone.

November 26.—Received order to go to Mud Geyser with pack mule and four pairs snowshoes.

November 27.—Left Fort Yellowstone for Norris; left post at 3 p. m , arrived Norris 7.30 p. m. Weather cold and storming. Saw 19 elks 6 miles south of post; also 2 deer and 3 coyotes 6½ miles south of post.

November 28.—Left Norris 10.30 a. m. for Mud Geyser; arrived Mud Geyser 4.30 p. m. Took Sergeant Welsh and Private Helm to assist me to Canyon Junction, but finding my horse and mule and Sergeant Simons's horse very tired, decided to have them go to Mud Geyser with me and return the following day via Canyon Hotel to see if it was possible to make a trip due north to Fort Yellowstone from Grebe Lake. Saw a band of elk on east side of Yellowstone River between Trout Creek and Mud Geyser; presume there were about 70 of them. Weather clear, until evening it began to snow.

November 29.—Left Mud Geyser on return trip to Norris with Sergeant Welsh and Private Helm. Went to Canyon Hotel to see how deep snow was, but found it too deep to go to Grebe Lake with horses. Went to hotel and sent Captain Erwin, the assistant superintendent of the park, the following message over telephone:

"Trip must be made on snowshoes. Leave Canyon; will be at Norris about 4 p. m. If any other orders call Norris.

" WHITTAKER, *Scout.*"

Did not arrive at Norris until 5 p. m. Weather forenoon cloudy, afternoon snowing very hard. Hard for stock to travel and make time.

November 30.—Stayed at Norris to wait for wagon to come with snowshoes. During the day I took Sergeant Welsh and Private Hemstead with their skis and broke the trail as far as Virginia Meadows; made a circuit of about 7 miles; found it very hard snowshoeing; the snow was very soft and our skis would sink about 6 to 8 inches. Wagon arrived at 5 p. m. with skis for Norris station and myself and Scout Malin. Weather very stormy.

December 1.—Sergeant Welsh, Scout Malin, and myself left Norris on snowshoes for Canyon Hotel at 9.45 a. m., arrived at Canyon at 3.30 p. m.; found snowshoeing fairly good for time of year. Depth of snow from 18 to 30 inches between Norris and Canyon Hotel. One mountain lion track on Canyon road 1 mile east of Norris; one on sulphur beds 3 miles west of Canyon. Met lineman and Privates Murphy and Davis on their way to Norris to get some mail which was brought out on the wagon yesterday; they return to Mud Geyser to-morrow. I sent my horses in from Norris by Private Hemstead. No game seen. Weather clear.

December 2.—Left Canyon Hotel with Sergeant Welsh and Scout Malin to make a trip to Grebe Lake, thence north to Fort Yellowstone, on snowshoes. Left Canyon Hotel at 8.35 a. m.; went up Cascade Creek to lake, thence to Grebe Lake; found all beaver had not been molested. Cut north from Grebe Lake and went to poachers' old cabin on the head waters of a tributary of Lava Creek. Saw no game. Snowshoeing was very easy to-day. Made about 10 miles from Canyon Hotel. Depth of snow, from 12 to 24 inches up to Grebe Lake; from there the snow was from 3 to 4 feet. Weather clear; 10 degrees below zero this morning at 6.30 o'clock.

December 3.—Left cabin with Sergeant Welsh and Malin at 7.30 a. m.; began to climb the divide and kept working along the top until we came to Storm Peak, then began to descend to Lupine Creek; when we reached the creek bed, we found it very hard shoeing on account of lack of snow. On the divide from the cabin all the way to Lupine Creek the snow was about 4 to 5 feet deep. No sign of anybody in that district. There seems to be a great many pine marten around Storm Peak and on the head waters of Lupine Creek; great many elk sign near Wraith Falls. I think we made about 25 miles on our trip for to-day. Weather clear and cold. Came in on foot from top of East Gardiner grade; arrived at post about 7.30 p. m. Saw 3 deer and 1 elk near Blacktail Creek; saw tepee near Storm Peak, but nothing in it. From the divide above cabin could see the Tower Creek country, but saw no sign of anything there.

[N. J. Malin, 1897.]

October 8.—Left Fort Yellowstone with Corporal Ornis and Private Canovan at 2.30 p. m.; arrived at Blacktail Creek at 5 p. m., about 8 miles east from fort. Saw 1 blacktail buck and 2 coyotes on the road.

October 9.—Went on; followed down Blacktail Creek near the mouth; beaver houses and dams had not been disturbed on the creek. I showed Ornis and Canovan the trail to cross the river at mouth of Blacktail; also lower and middle trail going to Cooke City. Camped at Yancey's about 5 p. m. No game seen. Weather very stormy; snow and wind.

October 10.—Left camp at Yancey's at 7.30. Crossed main Yellowstone on Baronett's bridge; then went up Lamar River about 1 mile and forded; then cut across divide to trail on north side of the river, leading to Cooke City, about 2¼ miles from Slough Creek; then turned northwest to Buffalo Plateau and made camp near Montana-Wyoming line on a branch of Hell Roaring Creek, 4 p. m. Corporal Herb and Private Hardin came to our camp near 5 p. m.—trailed us from where we hit the trail, on north side of Yellowstone, which leads to Soda Butte and Cooke City.

October 11.—Left camp with Ornis, Herb, and Canovan at 8.30 and traveled east to the pass between Hell Roaring and Buffalo Fork of Slough Creek. Found snow about 18 inches deep and crusted hard, so it was hard for horses to travel; then traveled north to what is considered near the north line of the park. Saw 1 blacktail buck and 4 bull elk; also beaver dam and house and fresh work of the beaver in the creek, which was a small branch of Hell Roaring. Herb sent Harding back to station. Snowing and cold; windy.

October 12.—Traveled north with Ornis, Herb, and Canovan, to north line near Hell Roaring Creek. Saw 5 bull elk on trip. Got back to camp at 5 p. m. Found Harding in camp.

October 13.—Ornis, Herb, and Harding scouted up the main Hell Roaring Creek; reported when returning no sign of game or poachers. I went west on Buffalo Plateau; no sign of game or poachers. Snowing and rain.

October 14.—All left camp at 10.30 a. m. and traveled main trail to Soda Butte. Got to station at 5 p. m.

October 15.—Left station at 10 a. m. with Ornis, Herb, and Bremer. Arrived at upper end of Alastin meadows at 5.30 p. m., about 2 miles south of the line of the park. Richard Randall and Roseborough in the party; they had written permit to carry their guns and to pack meat through the park to Soda Butte, thence along the road to Gardiner. Saw near 1,000 elk on Warm Spring Creek; also a very large band on Specimen Mountain.

October 16.—I took Herb, Bremer, Ornis, and Canovan as near north boundary line as I could judge from the line of Montana and Wyoming. Randall and Roseborough went across the line hunting. Clear and fine.

October 17.—All scouted up Slough Creek to where the line crosses the mountains. Clear and fine.

October 18.—Canovan and myself went across the point of the mountain to Buffalo Fork of Slough Creek to near line of park. The other men went up Slough Creek outside the park, hunting. Ornis killed a blacktail deer. Clear and fine.

October 19.—Started back to Soda Butte Station and arrived at 3.30 p. m. Roseborough and Randall also went to the Butte. Warm; thawing, so the travel was muddy.

October 20.—All remained at the station. Raining all day. Blane and Hoppe captured negro supposed to be the negro who broke jail in Deadwood, Dak.
October 21.—All left station for Cache Creek; followed up the main creek to right-hand fork, thence up the right-hand fork to the canyon, then up the divide to near the line of the park. Camped at 5 p. m. Herb, Ornis, Canovan, and Edwards, Randall, and Roseborough started east, hunting. I went on top of the mountain, so I could see Saddle Mountain and Baronet Peak, to determine, as near as possible, where the line would cut the mountain and creek, and found that we were camped in the park about three-quarters of a mile, as near as I could tell. Herb and Edwards, while hunting, came across the corner of the timber reserve, and found the line of the park; also trees and monuments showing the line. The line is also blazed as far as followed north and south. No sign of game in the country.
October 22.—Started back to station; arrived at 3 p. m. Lots of elk on bottom between Lamar River and Soda Butte Creek. I saw several coyotes and some mountain-lion tracks. Warm and pleasant.
October 23.—Randall, Ornis, Canovan, and I left station at 10 a. m. and arrived at camp on Slough Creek at 4.50 p. m. Saw several thousand elk between Soda Butte and Slough Creek. Both sides of Lamar River alive with elk; as near as I could judge, must have been 7,000.
October 24.—All hunted north of line for camp meat, but nothing outside of the park lines but bulls. Found on my way to camp an old camp where poachers had been camped. Near the line they had left their camp outfit, cooking utensils, also three quarters of elk, hung up in the trees, about 500 yards from their camp.
October 25.—All scouted the country between the north line and Slough Creek to see if we could find any more signs of poachers, but found no camps made lately. The beaver in Slough Creek have not been disturbed.
October 26.—Left camp on Slough Creek and followed it down through the canyon to or near the mouth. Crossed the Lamar River and went to Yancey's place and camped for the night. Several hundred elk at mouth of Slough Creek; also, several hundred on Specimen Mountain and Little Specimen Creek. Ornis killed 1 coyote, and we saw lots of signs and several coyotes.
October 27.—Left camp at 8.30 and arrived at Fort Yellowstone at 2.30. Saw no game, but a large herd had come off of Mount Washburn and crossed the road, going towards the Yellowstone River, near Devils Gut.
November 30.—Left post for Norris Station at 11 a. m. with Sergeant Bernstein, mounted, and Donehue as teamster. Saw a band of near 200 elk on Swan Lake Flat; 2 coyotes on road near Crystal Springs; 24 geese on lake at 3-mile post from Norris. Met syndicate team, with driver and Andy Wold, on road to Springs. Arrived at Norris Station at 4.30 p. m. Ten to 12 inches of snow beyond Crystal Springs to Norris.
December 1.—Left Norris, with Whittaker and Sergeant Welsh, for Canyon on snowshoes at 9.45; arrived at the Canyon Hotel at 3.30. Snow would average about 20 inches deep.
December 2.—Left Canyon Hotel with Whittaker and Sergeant Welsh. Traveled up Cascade Creek to the lake, thence across to Grebe Lake; then took up the trail that Reeb and Smitzer took after the robbery, to the cabin built by poachers. Cascade Creek and Lake frozen and covered with snow, so could tell nothing regarding the beaver in the creek and lake. No sign of game or poachers; snow average about 3½ feet deep.
December 3.—All left cabin at about 7.30 a. m.; traveled to top of divide looking into Tower Creek, then followed along the head of the divide to the head of Lupine Creek, then down the creek to the open country, then across to the main road leading from Springs to Cooke City; arrived at Fort Yellowstone at 8 p. m.; snow 4 to 5 feet deep in mountains, very little in the open country.
December 5.—Made trip along north line back of Cinnabar, then followed around the foot of mountains to target ground, then down old road to Gardiner. Game seen on trip, about 250 antelope in foothills, 3 blacktail deer near old brickyard, 8 bull elk above target ground, 2 live and 8 dead coyotes.

[George Whittaker, 1897.]

December 4.—Reported to the commanding officer for duty.
December 5 and 6.—Doing post duty.
December 7.—Left Mammoth Hot Springs for Yancey's with saddle horse and 2 pack mules. Saw 2 mountain sheep on east end of Mount Everts; 4 elk on Blacktail, 82 one mile west of Yancey's, and 2 deer same place. Weather stormy.
December 8.—Left Yancey's and proceeded to Soda Butte Station. Saw large herd of elk near hot spring, 2 miles southeast of Yancey's—about 75 in the herd; 3 small herds about 1 mile north of the junction of Yellowstone and Lamar rivers, 27 in one herd, 64 in next one, and I will venture to say there were over 300 in the other herd.

Twelve bull elk near the Junction Butte; 59 on the southeast side of Junction Butte; 33 near Cedar Ford of Lamar River; large herd near the mouth of Slough Creek—can say there were between 200 and 300; large herd on the east side of Slough Creek—between 50 and 75; 4 deer on Little Specimen Creek; 11 elk on Specimen divide; large herd on west side of Druid Peak of about 100; some scattered all the way from Amethyst Creek to Soda Butte. Corporal Herb and 2 privates absent on patrol duty on Slough Creek. Weather stormy. Snowed about 5 inches of snow during the night. Saw 7 coyotes near carcass of dead elk, 1 mile from station.

December 9.—Left station on snowshoes for trip up Opal Creek, then over to head of Flint Creek, but broke one of my snowshoes at foot of Specimen Ridge, so had to return to station. Was too late to make the trip by the time I had secured new shoes, so had to abandon it. Corporal Herb promised to make the trip by next Tuesday. Saw 14 elk opposite station. Weather cloudy.

December 10.—Left Soda Butte with Corporal Herb and Scout Malin for Hellroaring Creek. Saw about 700 elk near Junction Meadow; 200 on Slough Creek; about 1,000 scattered around between the outlet of Lamar River and Hellroaring Creek; also between 400 and 500 on east side of Hellroaring; some on west side also, but could not see them very well; should say there were about 150 of them. Camped on the State line near Hellroaring Creek. Saw 1 dead elk on Slough Creek and 6 coyotes eating on his carcass. The elk had evidently been run down and killed by the 6 coyotes last night. It was a last spring calf and was in good condition. Weather fair. No sign of anyone in the country we came over.

December 11.—Left camp with Corporal Herb and Scout Malin. Game seen to-day was 6 large herds of elk—2 herds on east side of Hellroaring creek, 3 herds on west side, and 1 herd on Blacktail Creek. It would be almost impossible to count them, but 1 will say there were at least 3,000 between Hellroaring and the mouth of Cottonwood Creek and 300 on Blacktail. Saw 3 white-tail deer near east side of Cottonwood Basin, 12 on Gardiner Grade, 1 mountain sheep near Cottonwood. No sign of anybody in the district.

Corporal Herb and his detachment keep a very close watch of that country. Corporal Herb came as far as Blacktail bridge, then left me and went to Yancey's. Malin left me at ford on Yellowstone River. Weather stormy. There were a great many fresh signs of beaver in Blacktail creek about 1 mile from outlet. Arrived at Fort Yellowstone at 4.45.

December 12.—Doing duty at Fort Yellowstone.

December 13.—Left post, mounted, with Private Dawson, of D Troop, and Private Martin, of H Troop, and 3 pack mules, for Fawn Pass. Proceeded as far as Golden Gate, where we were compelled to return to post on account of deep snowdrift in the gate, which was about 15 feet deep on the upper side and tapered down to 7 feet on lower side. Saw 10 deer at 3-mile post south of post. Weather very stormy.

December 19.—Left Fort Yellowstone with Scout Morrison and 4-mule team and driver at 8.10 a. m. for Norris. Had 4-mule team and 8 men to assist our team through the Snow Pass. After getting on the main road at Swan Lake found it fairly good traveling to Indian Creek; began to get very hard from there on; could not get farther than Crystal Spring on account of mules being tired; had to camp there for the night. Saw small herd of elk near the Snow Pass. Weather clear and cold.

December 20.—Left Crystal Spring cabin for the Canyon Hotel at about 8 a. m.; arrived at Norris for dinner. Left Norris at 2 p. m.; arrived at Canyon Hotel at 7.30 p. m. No game on road. Weather clear and cold.

December 21.—Left Canyon Hotel at 6.45 a. m., intending to go to Mud Geyser Station and secure the body of Private Davis, who was found frozen to death 10 miles from Lake Hotel on road to Thumb, and brought to Mud Geyser Station by Sergeants Simons and Welch and Private Akers. Found that Sergeants Simons and Welsh had tied the body up with canvas and had everything ready to start back to the Canyon Hotel after dinner. Left Mud Geyser at 1 p. m. with Scout Morrison, Sergeants Simons and Welsh and Private Hemstead to return to Canyon Hotel with body of Private Davis. Arrived at Canyon Hotel at 5 p. m. No game seen on road. Weather stormy in forenoon and clear in afternoon. Fairly good traveling for the team.

December 22.—Left Canyon Hotel at 7.25 a. m. for Crystal Spring; arrived at Norris for noon hour; left Norris 1.45 p. m.; arrived Crystal Spring at 5 p. m. Weather clear and cold.

December 23.—Left Crystal Spring with same party for Mammoth Hot Springs; left cabin at 7.04 a. m.; arrived Mammoth Hot Springs 11.55 a. m. Saw 17 elk near Snow Pass. Weather clear and cold. Depth of snow from Norris to Indian Creek about 2 feet; from Norris to Canyon 3 to 4 feet; from Canyon to Mud Geyser from 12 to 30 inches; all the snow is very soft.

December 24.—Left Fort Yellowstone to make a trip to Gardiner, Horr, and Aldridge; arrived at Gardiner; decided to remain over night. Weather cloudy.

December 25.—Left Gardiner City at 8.45 a. m., and proceeded to Horr. Stopped two hours in Horr, then proceeded to Aldridge; arrived there 12.30 p. m. Weather cloudy.

December 26.—Left Aldridge and returned to Gardiner. Remained in Gardiner over night. Weather stormy.

December 27.—Left Gardiner; from Gardiner went up on Mount Everts; saw a great many elk and antelope up there; saw 6 mountain sheep also; weather cold and stormy; from Mount Everts returned to Fort Yellowstone; arrived at post at 5.30 p. m. On this entire trip I have gathered some information that sooner or later will lead to the arrest of some poachers.

December 31.—Left Fort Yellowstone, mounted, with privates Disbrow and Root, of H Troop. Proceeded as far as Snow Pass, mounted; then proceeded on skis up Glen Creek; then over the divide to head of Gardiner River, at foot of Electric Peak, and camped for the night. Saw 12 elk near head of Glen Creek. Weather clear and cold.

[Geo. Whittaker, 1898.]

January 1.—Left camp with same party for Mulharen Creek and Fish Lake. Camped on Fish Lake over night. Saw one fresh track of mountain sheep. Weather clear.

January 2.—Left Fish Lake at daybreak. Proceeded down Mulharen Creek one mile; then kept working along the park line, intending to go to head of Reese Creek, but Private Root broke one of his snowshoes when we were just opposite Aldridge, so I had to go to the nearest road, as we could not use our skis any more. Saw one old snow trail, which I presume was one week old or more. Came on to an old cabin, but it was empty and there had been nobody near it this winter. The cabin is in the park, but very near the line. Saw no game. Weather clear. We arrived at Mammoth Hot Springs at 2 a. m. on the morning of the 3d.

January 12.—Sergeant Wall, of H Troop, and Corporal Herb, of Soda Butte Station, and myself left Fort Yellowstone for main camp on Big Blacktail Creek. From post we went to first bridge on Gardiner River, then turned to the right and went up the old road to old coal mine. At the coal mine we saw 22 mountain sheep—7 rams and 15 ewes. I then sent Corporal Herb on top of Mount Everts, while Sergeant Wall and I patrolled along the cliffs at Eagles Nest; then went down as far as the Yellowstone River; then up the old Turkey Pen road to Blacktail. Saw 1 mountain sheep near old slaughterhouse on Turkey Pen road; about 20 antelope on Gardiner flat. Saw about 1,200 elk on Mount Everts; saw 21 deer scattered on Mount Everts. Corporal Ornes and Private Bremier left post with pack train with rations and forage for main camp. Found everything O. K. in camp. Weather clear and very cold. Saw one human foot track on Everts, but it was about four days old and was not very plain.

January 13.—Took Sergeant Wall and Corporal Ornes, mounted, and proceeded up Crevasse Creek to patrol that place and also measure the distance from park line to where Miner killed the elk, and found it was 235 yards due south of the line, as near as we could make it. Brought the head to camp to be sent to post as evidence against Mr. Miner. Saw 88 elk on east side of Crevasse Creek; 24 on head of Dry Gulch creek. Weather cloudy.

January 14.—Left camp with Sergeant Wall and Corporal Herb and 3 pack mules to go over to Buffalo Creek and remain there three days, if necessary. Sent Corporal Ornes into the post with 2 mules and letter to Captain Erwin, and elk meat and elk head of Mr. Miner's. Saw 48 elk on Dry Gulch Creek; 4 white-tail deer same place. Elk sign were very numerous on Crevasse Mountain. Weather clear. Went into camp on Buffalo Creek at 4 p. m. The snow is very deep on Crevasse Mountain.

January 15.—Stayed in camp until about 11 a. m., then took Sergeant Wall and rode out toward the park line. Just before we came to the line we found an elk, dressed and covered with a blanket, and there was a fresh track of a man leading into the park, but before we got there he had come out again and gone down towards Bear Gulch, but later on I saw him coming back. I had already found his camp and a man in it who said his partner was out hunting horses, so I sent Corporal Herb down to watch his partner, when he came in, and see what he had with him. At that time I saw a man moving along the cliffs near the Yellowstone River, so I watched him until I thought he was in the park, then went after him and arrested him for hunting in the park. It turned out to be Scotty Crawford, or "Horse-thief Scotty." Brought him into the post and Captain Erwin ordered him confined until we could find out for certain whether he was in the park or not. Weather cloudy and cold.

January 16.—Left post with Lieutenant Arnold and proceeded to Buffalo Creek, to determine whether Scotty Crawford was in the park when we arrested him. Found the stakes and monuments and found that he (Scotty) was all of 50 yards out, but found where he had been all of 400 yards inside, but when arrested he was about 100 yards outside the line. Returned to Fort Yellowstone at 7.30 p. m. Weather clear and cold.

January 17.—Stayed at Fort Yellowstone to meet Sheriff Young from Livingston. He arrived on the mail stage and said he would take charge of Scotty in Gardiner, to morrow. Told him I would meet him at 10 a. m. Weather cloudy, not very cold.

January 18.—By order of Captain Erwin, took prisoner Crawford to Gardiner and turned him over to Sheriff Young, who told me to have all the witnesses to appear in Horr at 2 o'clock p. m. I sent Private Root up to camp and told him to have Sergeant Wall and Corporal Herb come down at once and move the camp down also. They arrived at 2 p. m. in Gardiner; then I took them to Horr. Scotty was tried and found "not guilty." Then his partner had Sergeant Wall arrested for taking his gun away from him, but Sergeant Wall was discharged. Justice Erret said he could not make a case of it. Returned to post at 8.45 p. m. Weather clear and very cold. Saw 8 mountain sheep at Eagles Nest.

January 19.—Stayed at post to wait for Private Carter to come in from camp on Blacktail Creek; he arrived at 8.45 p. m.

January 20.—Left post, mounted, and rode over to Mount Everts. Saw 8 mountain sheep on Mount Everts; about 600 elk there also; 6 deer same place. Saw where somebody had built a small footbridge across the Gardiner River, near the mouth. Returned to post at 5 p. m. Weather clear and cold.

January 21.—Left post with Private Weston, of H Troop, mounted. Proceeded from the bridge 2 miles north of post to the old coal bank on Mount Everts; from there to mouth of Gardiner River, thence along the north line of park as far as the Gassert ranche, thence back to Fort Yellowstone. Saw 11 mountain sheep on Mount Everts; about 200 antelope on Gardiner flat on east side of the Gardiner River; 4 whitetail deer near Government garden; 7 near post ice house; about 75 elk back of the Gassert ranche. Arrived at post about 5.30 p. m. Weather clear and cold.

January 22.—Remained in post until 6 p. m., then packed up 5 mules and left post with Sergeant Wall, Private Weston, and Private Martin to make a night camp on Mount Everts. Made camp on McMahon Creek at 8.10 p. m. Returned to post with Private Martin at 9.20 p. m. Left Sergeant Wall and Private Weston of H Troop in camp for six days, by order of Captain Erwin. Weather stormy and cold.

January 23.—Left post, mounted, with Private Carter and Private Martin, of H Troop, and Private Squires, of D Troop, and 5 pack mules to make a camp just back of Cinnabar. Left post at 10 a. m.; arrived in camp at 1 p. m. Sent Private Martin back to post with 3 mules. Saw about 150 antelope on Gardiner Flat; 6 elk back of Gassert ranche. Weather, clear and cold.

January 24.—Left camp with Private Carter to make a patrol up Reese Creek. Left camp at 8.30 a. m.; returned at 4.30 p. m. After going up Reese Creek to within one-half mile of park line saw some smoke away up in a little draw or ravine and concluded it was a poachers camp. I went about one-fourth mile inside the park; saw lots of game sign. Tried to ride to foot of Electric Creek, but snow was too deep for our horses; so returned to camp to go up and get Sergeant Wall and Private Weston to come down and help me investigate what that camp is doing there. Weather very cold all day, and clear.

January 25.—Left camp with Private Squires and went up to Sergeant Wall's camp to get him to come down and assist me for one day to investigate camp fire seen yesterday on Reese Creek. When I got to Gardiner I was informed that the sergeant had gone over to Buffalo Creek; so decided to send Private Squires back to camp and I would wait in Gardiner for the return of Sergeant Wall. Saw about 50 antelope on Gardiner Flat. Sergeant Wall arrived from Buffalo Creek at 6.30 p. m. Weather clear and very cold; 18 below zero at Gardiner. Remained with Sergeant Wall over night.

January 26.—Left Sergeant Wall's camp with Sergeant Wall and Private Weston. Proceeded to within 1 mile of Cinnabar, then fired two shots as a signal for Private Carter to meet us in Cinnabar. Left Cinnabar at 11 a. m. and went up Reese Creek as far as the park line, thence along said line to the foot of Electric Peak, thence back to where I saw the smoke on the 21st. Found that where we saw the smoke there is an old man, who built a log cabin last fall. He is mining coal. His cabin is about 150 yards from park line. Saw where two elk or deer had been killed and dragged down Reese Creek to Horr, but they were killed outside the park. Also found an old bear trap just outside the park; it has been there for about one year. There seems to be a great many fresh elk sign on Reese Creek and all of them are inside the park. Sergeant Wall and Private Weston returned to their own camp this p. m. Weather cloudy and cold.

January 27.—Sent Private Carter up to help Sergeant Wall take out the footbridge across the Gardiner River. Left camp about 2 p. m. and rode up to foot of Sepulchre Mountain to see if any poaching had been done there, but saw no sign of any having been done there. Saw 32 elk at foot of Sepulchre Mountain. Private Carter returned at 5.30 p. m. from Sergeant Wall's camp. He informed me that the footbridge was taken out by Sergeant Wall and himself. He saw about 100 antelope on Gardiner Flat. Weather cloudy and very windy.

January 28.—Left camp with Private Squires to make a patrol up Reese Creek. As this is the day I am told to go to the post, thought that I had better make this patrol before going. Saw where an elk had been killed yesterday—but outside the Park—and dragged to Horr. Returned to camp about 5.30 p. m. and started to pack up and go to Sergeant Wall's camp and take him in also, but when we got there he had just returned from Buffalo Creek to look after Scotty's camp, and it being late and his stock tired, decided to remain there until morning and pull into the post by daybreak. My idea for doing this at night is to keep the hunting class of people thinking the camps were still out where they were. Weather clear and warm.

January 29.—Left camp on McMahon Creek with Sergeant Wall and Private Carter and Private Weston, of H Troop, and Private Squires, of D Troop, at 6.30 a. m. for Fort Yellowstone. Saw about 100 antelope on west slope of Mount Everts; 2 elk and 11 mountain sheep same place. Arrived at post at 8 a. m. Weather clear and very cold. Reported for duty at 9.30 a. m.

[Sergt. M. J. Wall, Troop H, Fourth Cavalry.]

January 23—Left camp at 10 a. m. Made a patrol on Mount Everts on the southeast slope, with Sergeant Wall and Private Weston. Game seen during patrol, about 100 head of elk and 6 blacktail deer. On the east of Mount Everts discovered an elk killed by a mountain lion, lying south from my camp. Saw tracks about one day old of man and horses passed by my camp and going towards Gardiner. Distance traveled, about 20 miles. Weather very cold.

January 24.—Left camp at 8.30 a. m. Patrolled Turkey Pen Trail with Private Weston. Game seen, 200 head of antelope on Gardiner Flat and 100 head of elk near my camp on the mountain east of Turkey Pen Trail. Saw 3 mountain sheep, and on south of trail saw 200 head of elk. On my return saw man's tracks leading from Gardiner to the ridge south of Yellowstone River; lost his trail in the rocks, and saw one mountain sheep, a ram, which looked to me as if he was hunted. Waited for signs of something to turn up and could find nothing, so returned to camp. Distance traveled, about 25 miles. Weather cold and clear.

January 25.—Left camp at 8.30 a. m. Made a patrol to Buffalo Creek with Private Weston. Game seen during patrol, 100 head of antelope on Gardiner Flat, east of Gardiner River. Found Crawford's camp on Buffalo Creek; went to his camp; spoke to him about the meat that was lying on trail; he said he knew nothing about it. Left his camp and went to the line. Found fresh tracks leading into the park; tracks that were made by a man's foot. Returned to McMahon Creek. Distance traveled, about 25 miles. Weather very cold.

January 26.—Left camp at 9 a. m. Made a patrol of the northern boundary with Scout Whittaker, Private Weston, and Private Carter. Game seen during patrol, about 150 head of antelope on Gardiner Flat and 15 head of elk outside of the line, northwest of Electric Peak. Found the camp that Scout Whittaker thought to be Bucher's was an old prospector's cabin. Was told by a rancher named McMahon that there was deer taken out on Monday (24th) by coal miners. Returned to McMahon Creek. Weather cloudy and cold. Distance traveled, about 20 miles.

January 28.—Left camp at 10 a. m. A patrol made to Gardiner River. Game on Gardiner Flat, 200 head of antelope. Met Private Carter on the side of river; had him help, myself, and Private Weston to cut the footbridge across the Gardiner River. After the bridge was cut went on Turkey Pen Trail. Saw 200 head of elk on east of trail. Returned to camp. Weather windy and cold. Distance traveled, about 15 miles.

January 28.—Left camp at 9.30 a. m. Patrol east of Mount Everts with Private Weston. Game seen on and around Mount Everts, about 600 head of elk and 6 blacktail deer on McMahon Creek, 1 mountain lion on the east side of Mount Everts hunting elk, but when he saw us coming towards him he made for cover. After making this patrol went to Crawford's camp. Found fresh trails leading to the park; too late to follow them, so returned to camp. Weather clear and cold. Distance traveled, about 28 miles.

January 29.—Left camp at 6.30 a. m. Game seen on return to post, 100 head of antelope and 10 mountain sheep on south of Everts. Built a cabin on McMahon Creek.

[George Whittaker, 1898.]

January 4.—Left the post, mounted, and took in all the country at the foot of Sepulchre Mountain down as far as the corner of Chadbourne's ranche; then came back by way of Gardiner City. Saw 4 elk near the target range, about 110 antelope near Gardiner, 5 white-tail deer in Government garden, 12 near Government ice house. Weather clear and very warm.

January 5.—Left Fort Yellowstone with Corporal Ornes, of D Troop, and Private Carter, of H Troop, mounted; took five pack mules and proceeded to mouth of Blacktail Creek and went into camp there, so I could scout all the Crevasse Mountain country. Saw one man on snowshoes; sent Corporal Ornes after him; found out he was coming from Cooke City on his way to Gardiner. He had a pistol, but was sealed at Soda Butte. Saw a great many elk on Blacktail Deer Creek. The beaver in this creek have done a great deal of work, but are not working now. They have not been molested so far this winter. Weather cloudy and very wintry, but not cold.

January 6.—Left camp with Corporal Ornes and left Private Carter in camp; decided to go down the river to J. S. Knowles's ranch and see what was going on there, then go up on Crevasse Mountain and see if there is any poaching going on there; got to J. S. Knowles's cabin; found there was nobody at home; looked around for any elk meat that might be stored there, but found none. We then proceeded up Crevasse Creek; there we found two human footprints in the snow; followed them around to park line. The country was all pawed up by elk; there must have been hundreds of them in there last week, but they have been shot at and they have all moved back into Cottonwood Basin, except 11 that we saw to-day, and they ran for that place as soon as they saw us coming. After going to park line we began to circle a radius of 500 yards to see what those two men had been doing. I found where a quarter of elk had been cached overnight; I suppose it had been dragged there from the cache to Tom Miner's cabin. I followed the trail where it had been dragged, and it led to Tom Miner's door; am going back on the 8th to see just where it was killed; looked to-day as far as the park line, but could not find the carcass. Tom Miner told me, when I asked him who had dragged the meat, that he had, and that he was going to drag some more just as soon as he could get to kill one. My opinion is that he did not kill the elk, but somebody has killed several elk somewhere on Crevasse Creek and gave him the front quarters, for when I got to his cabin he was out and I looked into his meat house, but saw nothing but fore quarters and one old hind quarter of elk or deer; I did not take time to note which. Saw 3 whitetail deer near J. S. Knowles's cabin. Knowles was at home on my return, and so was Miner. Weather, very stormy.

January 7.—Left camp and rode to south end of Cottonwood Basin to meet Corporal Herb, but he failed to come, so returned to camp. Saw 3 whitetail deer and 97 elk to-day along the Yellowstone River. Weather, clear.

January 8.—Left camp with Corporal Ornes, proceeded to Tom Miner's cabin. Requested Miner to go with us and show us where he had killed his elk. At first he refused to do so, but after talking to him a little while he concluded to go. Found that he had first shot the elk outside the park about 500 yards, but the elk ran into the park about 400 yards before he killed it, so he killed the elk inside the park, but wounded it outside, for which I feel that I am in duty bound to arrest him for the offense. Saw a great many herds of elk on Crevasse Mountain near the park line, but they were all inside the park. Two whitetail deer above Miner's cabin. After we got through at Miner's we proceeded to Buffalo Creek, arrived there at sundown. Weather very cold and cloudy. Sent Private Carter into the post with 3 pack mules and note to Captain Erwin.

January 9.—Left camp on Buffalo Creek on foot; went out about half a mile, but it was snowing so hard that we could see nothing whatever, so decided to return to camp and listen for any shooting that might take place, but did not hear any near the park line, except below Gardiner we could hear six shots fired just at dusk and one in the forenoon. Heard two shots fired on Mount Everts about 5.30 p. m. Have seen no sign of anyone having been in the park poaching, except Tom Miner on Crevasse Creek. Saw no game to-day. Weather, stormy; snowing hard all day.

January 10.—Left camp on Buffalo Creek to return to camp on Big Blacktail Creek. Saw no sign of anyone poaching in the park. Got back to Tom Miner's cabin and found him dressing up to leave. I told I would have to arrest him for killing elk in the park. Took him to our camp on Big Blacktail and kept him overnight. Saw a great many elk on Crevasse Mountain, but outside the park. Weather, clear.

January 11.—Left camp on Blacktail for Fort Yellowstone with Corporals Herb and Ornes and prisoner Miner. (Corporal Herb met me on Crevasse Creek on the 10th instant.) Left Mr. Miner's arms and meat in camp, pending action of the commanding officer at the post. Saw 117 elk near mouth of Blacktail and 40 between Blacktail and top of Gardiner grade; 9 blacktail deer on Gardiner grade, 14 at forks of East and West Gardiner rivers; 9 mountain sheep on Mount Everts, opposite same place; 5 deer east corner of pasture. Arrived at the post with prisoner at 1 p. m. Weather, cloudy and very cold.

January 30.—Left post with Sergeant Wall, Private Weston, Private Martin, and 5 pack mules, to put Sergeant Wall in camp on McMahon Creek, on Mount Everts, by order of Captain Erwin. Returned to post with Private Martin and pack mules. Weather, clear.

January 31.—Received orders from Captain Erwin to take 2 privates and 3 pack mules to make a six days' trip to the Soda Butte district and Crevasse Mountain, then return to the post. Weather, clear.

February 1.—Left post with Private Martin, Private Rompre, of H Troop, Private Slough of D Troop, and 4 pack mules, for Hellroaring Creek. Only got as far as outlet of Big Blacktail Creek, on account of the ice in the Yellowstone River, which was frozen out so far from shore that we had to cut a channel through. Camped in old camp at ford of river. Saw two mountain sheep on east point of Mount Everts; got within 30 feet of large ram near the Cooke City road. Saw about 1,000 elk scattered along the road from top of Gardiner grade to mouth of Blacktail Creek. The beaver in Blacktail have not been working lately, nor have they been molested. Clear.

February 2.—Left camp with Privates Rompre and Slough to go up to Soda Butte Station, via Hellroaring and Slough Creeks. Sent Private Martin back to post with 1 mule. Saw about 3,000 elk between Cottonwood Creek and Soda Butte; 3 whitetail deer, 1 blacktail deer; 1 mountain sheep near Cottonwood Creek. Found 3 men absent on patrol duty when I arrived at station, but they returned at 8.15 p. m. Weather, clear.

February 3.—Left station with same party and returned to camp at Blacktail Ford with rations for the brush cabin on Line Creek. On Hellroaring Creek found everything O. K. at the station. Saw about 1,000 elk on Hellroaring, about 700 of them in one herd. Saw 9 mountain sheep near Cottonwood Creek; 3 whitetail deer near the ford of Yellowstone River. Weather, blinding snowstorms for about four hours and very cloudy all day. Average depth of snow 15 inches from Hellroaring to Soda Butte Station.

February 4.—Stayed in camp at Blacktail Ford of the Yellowstone River to fix up brush cabin and listen for any shooting on Crevasse Mountain. Our stock was very tired from our trip to Soda Butte and back here, which is about 28 miles each way. The ice in the river has about all gone out in the last two days. Weather, cloudy in a. m., clear in p. m.

February 5.—Left camp with same party and proceeded to J. S. Knowles's cabin, thence over Crevasse Mountain to Buffalo Creek, to look after Scotty's camp and see what he is doing there. We arrived on Buffalo Creek Mountain about 1.30 p. m. Went into camp inside the park line. Laid low all the afternoon to listen for any shooting that might take place, but did not hear any. Saw an old web snowshoe trail leading into the park from Scotty's camp, but it was three or four days old. Saw where one elk had been shot inside the park, but could not see where it had been butchered. Saw 3 whitetail deer at Knowles Lake, 4 at Knowles Cabin; 42 elk on Crevasse Mountain about 100 yards outside the park. Weather, cloudy and chinook wind blowing.

February 6.—Left camp with same party; went out on the cliffs and watched for anyone coming out or going into the park. Stayed there until about 1 p. m., then went over to my old camp on Buffalo Creek. Found that Scotty had camped there since his arrest, but he has moved away in the last three or four days. I have since been informed that he has moved down the river about 4 miles below Gardiner. After finding he had moved I came over to Sergeant Wall's camp on McMahon Creek; found Sergeant Wall and Private Weston absent on patrol duty. There has not been much of anything going on since January 15. Weather, cloudy and chinook wind. Saw no game.

February 7.—Left camp with Sergeant Wall and made a patrol down to Reese Creek. There has been some elk killed, but outside the park. Privates Weston and Rompree made a patrol over Mount Everts. Private Slough remained in camp. They saw 8 elk and 30 antelope on Mount Everts. We left camp at 6 p. m. for the post; arrived at post at 7.30 p. m. Weather, cloudy and warm wind.

[Sergeant M. J, Wall, 1898.]

January 30.—Left the post at 6.15 p. m.; made camp on McMahon Creek at 8.20 p. m. Night mild.

January 31.—Left camp at 10.20 a. m. Made a patrol on Gardiner Flat. Found Tom Newcomb on Gardiner Flat and told him the commanding officer wanted to see him. Returned to camp and made a patrol on the east side of Mount Everts. Game seen: 100 antelope on the east side of Mount Everts, 6 mountain sheep, same side, and 20 elk on the west side of McMahon Creek. Weather, warm. Traveled about 10 miles.

February 1.—Left camp at 10 a. m. Made a patrol on Turkey Pen Trail and on the east side of Mount Everts. Game seen, 150 antelope on Gardiner Flat, and 200 head of elk counted on northeast side of McMahon Creek, and 1 mountain sheep (a ram) on the mountain northeast of the Turkey Pen Trail, and about 400 elk on the south slope of Mount Everts. Discovered one blacktail deer, killed by a mountain lion, on the east side of Mount Everts about 100 yards from where he killed the elk. I saw his tracks in a great many places, and believe he is about as big as an African lioness. I saw 5 bull elk south of McMahon Creek. They were all very large. I saw Tom Newcomb on Gardiner Flat, and he gave me a bottle of strychnine to put on the meat, which I did. No signs of anyone having been on Mount Everts since last patrol. Weather, fine and mild. Traveled about 20 miles.

February 2.—Left camp at 8.30 a. m. Made a patrol on Buffalo Creek and Buffalo Mountain with Private Weston. Found Crawford's camp to be abandoned. Looked all around Buffalo Creek and Buffalo Mountain, but he was not to be found in that location; he must have left camp on the 31st of January, in the night. I saw his camp on that day from Mount Everts. There was a man walking on Buffalo Mountain. Saw fresh man and horse's tracks leading from Crawford's camp to Mr. Moore's cabin; I believe them to be the tracks of Crawford. There is a cabin on the northeast of Buffalo Mountain, where there was someone, but seeing me coming they left. I had heard a shot fired long before I got there. When I reached the place I saw about 100 head of elk all around Buffalo Mountain, looking as if they were hunted very much. Followed trails all around and could find no signs of any game having been killed, so returned to camp. Game seen during patrol: 200 antelope on Gardiner Flat and on the east slope of Mount Everts; about 200 elk on east and west of Buffalo Mountain. Weather, normal. Traveled about 25 miles.

February 3.—Left camp at 9.30 a. m. Made a patrol on the north boundary line and to Reese Creek and to a prospector's cabin; no signs of anyone having been there of late. I had Private Weston patrol the east of Mount Everts and look at the deer that was poisoned. He found two foxes, which were poisoned, and were destroyed by crows picking holes in their heads; he also saw 30 bull elk on the south slope of Mount Everts and 400 cow elk on the east slope of Mount Everts, and 4 mountain sheep on the ridge of Everts. Game seen during the day: 100 head of antelope on Gardiner Flat and 50 head of elk on the west side of McMahon Creek, and 6 mountain sheep on the east of Mount Everts. Weather, blowing northwest and light snow. Traveled about 20 miles.

February 4.—Left at 9 a. m. Made a patrol on Crevasse Mountain to meet Scout Whittaker, which I failed to do on account of snowdrifts. My patrol would be to Mr. Knowles's cabin to leave a note for the scout. Also my horse was very lame and could not make it to Mr. Knowles's cabin and then to my camp, so I returned to camp. On my return I saw the poachers' cabin on Buffalo Mountain. I went over to it. There was a fire burning inside, but no one at home. I looked all around and saw some mink skins and what I thought to be fox skins. Waited to see if anyone would show up; then it was getting dark, so I returned to camp. Game seen, 200 antelope on Gardiner Flat. Private Weston made a patrol on Turkey Pen Trail, and also went to the top of the mountain northeast of Turkey Pen Trail. He saw 11 mountain sheep on the mountain. Two of them he said were rams, which he said were last spring lambs, and the remainder of them very small. He also stated that he believes all the big rams are killed off. Private Weston saw 200 elk west of Turkey Pen Trail and 100 antelope on Gardiner Flat. I believe there is more poaching done around here than any other part of the park, outside of Snake River and Riverside. There is a variety of game in this part—1,000 elk, 300 antelope, 200 blacktail deer, about 40 mountain sheep, and plenty of foxes, beaver, and mink. Weather, fair. Traveled about 30 miles.

February 5.—Private Weston left camp at 9.30 a. m.; made a patrol on the north boundary line and to Reese Creek. Said he saw no signs of anyone having been there since last patrolled. Game seen during his patrol, about 200 antelope on Gardiner Flat, 1 that was crippled on the west side of Gardiner River, 20 head of elk on Reese Creek, and 15 blacktail deer on Reese Creek. He traveled about 15 miles.

I left camp on the same day about 11 a. m.; made a patrol on Turkey Pen Trail and on Mount Everts. Travel very bad on account of snowdrifts. Game seen during patrol, about 40 elk on the slope south of McMahon Creek, 7 blacktail deer on the ridge of Mount Everts, and 6 mountain sheep on the west of Mount Everts. Found 1 fox that had died from the poisoned deer meat. No signs of anyone having been there since last patrol. Weather, mild. Traveled about 10 miles.

February 6.—Left camp at 9 a. m.; made a patrol on Turkey Pen Trail and to Cooke City road. Game seen, about 200 elk on the west side of trail and 1 mountain sheep on the mountain northeast of the trail, and about 200 antelope on Gardiner Flat. Sent Private Weston to the post to get one day's rations. No signs of anyone over the trail since last patrol. Weather, chinooky. Traveled about 16 miles.

February 7.—Left camp at 9.30 a. m.; made a patrol on the north boundary line. Scout Whittaker and I saw signs of blood on the trail leading to the line of the park; looked as if it was meat that was taken but the night before. Saw fresh tracks of a man and horse leading to the park; heard one shot fired close to the line. Also made a patrol on Reese Creek. Saw no signs of anyone having been there since last patrol. Weather, chinooky. Traveled about 12 miles.

[Scout Whittaker, 1898.]

February 8.—Reported to Captain Erwin for duty. Attended court at Commissioner Meldrum's house—Tom Miner case.
February 9.—Attended court again on Tom Miner case. Weather, clear.
February 10.—Attended court until 11.30 a. m., when trial was over. Prisoner found guilty of killing an elk in the park. Took Private Martin and all the pack mules out in the afternoon for practice. Weather, clear.
February 11.—Left post, mounted, with Private Root to make a patrol along north line of park, via Gardiner and Cinnabar, and try to locate Scotty's camp; found it on Trail Creek. Returned to post at 5.30 p. m. Weather, cloudy.
February 12.—Remained in the post.
February 13.—Took Private Murphy and left post, mounted, to make a patrol on Mount Everts. Returned to post at 5.45 p. m. Weather, cloudy and very windy.
February 14.—Remained in the post.
February 15.—Left post with Sergeant Wall, mounted, to make a patrol to Buffalo Creek and Mount Everts. Returned to post about 4.45 p. m. Left Sergeant Wall out on Mount Everts until about 7 p. m., when he should return to the post. He returned about that time.
February 16.—Reported to Captain Erwin at 9 a. m. for orders, but it was storming so hard at that time could do nothing. Storm ceased about 10.30 a. m. Received orders at that time to take Sergeant Wall and Private Weston with seven days' rations and leave post after dinner. Left post at 2.30 p. m.; put Sergeant Wall in camp, and returned to post with the mules. Weather, very stormy.
February 17.—Remained in the post.
February 18.—Left post with Private Slough, of D Troop, and Privates La Mont and Martin, of H Troop, with five days' rations and five pack mules, to make a patrol to Hellroaring Creek. Saw about 300 elk between forks of Gardiner River and outlet of Big Blacktail Creek. The beaver in this creek have not been molested. Saw 3 deer on east end of Mount Everts; 6 deer on north side of Yellowstone River, opposite camp. The snow was not very deep, except a few drifts. Weather, cloudy.
February 19.—Stayed in camp until 12.30; then went up the river with Private Slough to look for sheep sign. Sent Privates La Mont and Martin back to post with 2 mules, Private La Mont to return to camp after they got to Blacktail Lake. He saw about 75 elk and 4 deer. Weather, clear.
February 20.—Left camp with Private Slough and Private La Mont, and went down to Crevasse Creek to see if any one had been there, but saw no sign of anything having been done there since I was there last time. Mr. Knowles informed me that there have been all of 2,000 elk in sight at one time near his place, in the last fifteen days. I saw 26 elk on the east side of Crevasse Creek, one-half mile north of Mr. Knowles', inside the park. The elk seem to be working up very high and back towards the Hellroaring district. Saw 14 deer, 6 whitetail and 8 blacktail on opposite side of the river from our camp. The snow is not very deep anywhere yet, except on Crevasse Mountain. Saw one scabby elk near the ford on Oxbow Creek. Weather, clear and very warm.
February 21.—Left camp with Private Slough and Private La Mont. Rode up to south end of Cottonwood Basin to look over the sheep range and see if they were still there, but after looking over it carefully I could not see a single fresh sign of any sheep. I presume the sheep have moved to some other range. Saw 5 whitetail deer near mouth of Cottonwood Creek. Saw about 1,000 elk between the ford and south end of Cottonwood Basin; also, found 3 calf elk that had been killed by mountain lion, there being fresh tracks of such animals around the carcass of each elk. Weather, stormy.
February 22.—When we woke up this morning we found all of our mules gone, but still had the troop horses left. We rode them after the mules, and found them about 2 miles from camp. Returned to camp, packed up, and proceeded to Sergeant Wall's camp. After we arrived there I received orders from Captain Erwin, through Private Weston, to investigate the killing of a deer about 1 mile above the Government ice lake. I found said deer and also the carcass of an elk. The deer had been shot, but the elk, in my opinion, had been killed by coyotes. I came into the post with Private Weston and Private La Mont, and reported the same to Captain Erwin, who gave me orders to remain in the post over night and return to Sergeant Wall's camp to-morrow morning, leaving Privates Weston and La Mont in the post. Saw 17 blacktail deer near mouth of Blacktail Creek, 6 on Mount Everts, 18 just above the Government ice lake. Saw about 250 elk on Mount Everts, and 7 coyotes same place. Weather, clear.

[Sergt. M. J. Wall, 1898.]

February 16.—Left camp at 4 p. m., to patrol the Gardiner Flat and portion of Turkey Pen. Found no signs of anyone crossing the Gardiner River. The antelope were on Gardiner Flat in small bands, from 10 to 15 in each band, and seemed to be more wild and uneasy than ever. On my return I crossed Gardiner River and found about 150 in one band on the west side of Gardiner River, about 400 yards from Gardiner City, very much watched by the so-called citizens of Gardiner. Two men had guns; one of them Mr. Mack, the other was a stranger to me. There was also about 300 head of elk on the northeast slope of Mount Everts. Weather, cold and light snow. Traveled about 10 miles.

February 17.—Left camp at 10.30 a. m., and patrolled Buffalo Creek and Buffalo Mountain, and followed boundary line to where it crosses the Yellowstone River. Myself and Private Weston went to the camp of Crawford, which was supposed to be occupied by John Dewing. It was found deserted, and there was no evidence of its having been used by anyone lately. The cabin on north side of Buffalo Mountain is still used by parties, but have found no evidence of game being killed across park line, nor no new trails leading into park. Saw 5 blacktail deer on Buffalo Creek and signs of elk on Buffalo Mountain. Returned to camp at 6 p. m. Weather, cold. Traveled about 16 miles.

February 18.—Left camp at 9.30 a. m., and patrolled Reese Creek and north boundary line, myself and Private Weston. On going through Gardiner, a man joined us on the road, and told me there were parties going in there, but if I would watch it that night I would catch them coming out. I afterwards found his name out and asked those men's names, which he said he did not care to tell. I also found out that he was putting me on the wrong trail. Game seen, 6 blacktail deer on the west side of Reese Creek and 1 cow elk, which was wounded in the shoulder. She was then traveling up Reese Creek. Weather, cold. Traveled about 15 miles.

February 19.—Left camp at 10 a. m. and patrolled Trail Creek Mountain with Private Weston; also to find Crawford's camp, but could not locate it. Was told he had taken a load of meat out to Horr, and on my return myself and Private Weston went to Horr to find out if it was so. I was told he was not bringing his meat to that town. I saw Crawford there on the same day. Game seen: About 250 elk on slope of Mount Everts and 200 antelope on the west side of Gardiner River. Returned to camp about 6.30 p. m. Traveled about 20 miles. Weather, cold.

February 20.—Left camp at 10 a. m. and patrolled Trail Creek and also went to the town of Horr. I had sent Private Weston to Mount Everts, to find out if he could see the sheep on the regular range, but he could not see any signs of them. He thinks they have left Mount Everts. When I got to Horr I saw the said Brundage, and Dewing, and Drummond (a man who is a stranger to me), and Brundage's pack horses standing outside Mr. Welcome's saloon. Brundage had made a remark to the strange man, "I am ready, as I am out of meat and money, and we must go to-night." I heard him say, "We will go towards Reese Creek." After they had left I sent a telegram to the post for two men to report to me at Horr. Sergeant Alexander and Private Palmer reported to me. We waited until towards morning, then left for Reese Creek. We patrolled every place we thought we could find them, but failed to do so; then we thought they were notified. Returned to camp about 7 a. m. and Sergeant Alexander and Private Palmer returned to post. Weather, cold. Traveled about 28 miles.

February 21.—Private Weston left camp at 7 a. m. Made a patrol on the north boundary line and also up towards Ice Lake. Hearing shots fired, he went in that direction, and found one blacktail deer dead, about 1½ miles southeast of Ice Lake. He returned to camp, and not finding me there, waited for my return. I was making a patrol on Gardiner Flat. When I returned he reported it to me. Game seen by Private Weston: 50 head of elk on the west side of Gardiner River. Game seen by myself: 12 head of antelope on Gardiner flat. Weather, fair. Private Weston traveled about 12 miles; I traveled 4 miles.

February 22.—Left camp at 9.30 a. m. with Private Weston. Went to the place where Weston had seen the dead deer. We thought the best thing to do was to skin the deer and send Private Weston to the post to report to the commanding officer, which he did. I waited around there for some time to see if anyone would show up, but no one came, so I returned to camp. On my return I found Scout Whittaker and his party in my camp, and Private Weston returned from the post, with orders from the commanding officer for all to return to the post. Scout Whittaker told me he would leave me and Private Slough in camp until further orders. Game seen: 200 antelope on the west side of Gardiner River. Weather, fine. Traveled 8 miles.

February 23.—Left camp at 11 a. m. On my way I met Private Martin, and he told me to report to Scout Whittaker, myself and Private Slough, which I did; and he told me to take Sergeant Alexander and Private Lefler to the place where the deer lay, which I did; and then I was to report to Scout Whittaker, to find out where all the shooting was done which we heard. We could not find out, so we returned to camp about 9.30 p. m. Game seen: About 200 antelope on west side of Gardiner River; 14 elk around Ice Lake. Weather, fine. Traveled about 18 miles.

February 24.—Packed up all property and sent Private Martin to the post with pack mules. I left camp at 10 a. m. to make a patrol to Horr, which I did, and meeting Mr. Welcome, he told me if I would lay for Brundage I would catch him. I returned to Cinnabar, and meeting Scout Whittaker, I reported to him what I had heard from Mr. Welcome. Scout Wittaker sent Private Slough to the post to find out what to do. Scout Whittaker told me to go as far as Mr. Shields's ranch and he would send me a man, which I did, and couldn't find any trail of Brundage, so I returned and found Scout Whittaker and Private Slough at Yellowstone Bridge, where Scout Morrison joined us shortly afterwards; then all returned to the post about midnight. Game seen: 7 blacktail deer. Weather, cold. Traveled about 30 miles.

[Scout Jas. G. Morrison, 1897 and 1898.]

November 24, 1897.—Left the post with Privates McReynolds and Miller to go over on the Gallatin. On account of deep snow we got no farther than the pocket on Fawn Creek, where we camped. Saw about 750 elk; also numerous signs of beaver on the Gardiner River and Fawn Creek. Distance traveled, about 12 miles.

November 25.—Took back trail down Fawn Creek about 4 miles; thence south along Quadrant Mountain to Indian Creek and up it about 4 miles to snowshoe shack, where we camped. Saw about 150 elk. Many signs of beaver on this creek. Distance traveled, about 15 miles.

November 26.—Remained in camp; scouting up Indian Creek. No signs of game. Distance traveled, about 10 miles.

November 27.—Proceeded to the post. Distance, 12 miles.

February 14, 1898.—Left the post, accompanied by Corporal Ornes and Private Rompre, at 9 a. m. for Soda Butte. Arrived at Yancey's at 4 p. m. Saw about 800 elk. Warm and snow. Distance, 20 miles.

February 15.—Left Yancey's at 9.30 a. m.; arrived at Soda Butte at 4 p. m. Saw about 500 elk. Distance traveled, 15 miles. Warm and pleasant.

February 16.—Remained at Soda Butte on account of very severe snowstorm. Warm and snow.

February 17.—Party, consisting of Corporals Ornes and Herb and Privates Edwards and Rompre, left station, mounted, for Mirror Plateau, following trail up East Fork of Yellowstone. The snow was too deep south of Miller Creek, so made camp south of it about one-fourth mile. Snow 2½ feet deep. Saw about 100 elk on north side of Cache Creek: a great number of Elk signs all the way up to Miller Creek. In Cache Creek bottom saw signs of blacktail deer, but saw only 1, a doe. Distance, 13 miles. Clear and very cold.

February 18.—Left camp with Corporals Ornes and Herb for Ponuntpa Springs on skis, following right bank of East Fork to within a mile of Timothy Creek, up Timothy to near its head, and camped. Snow about 3 feet, very loose, and skiing very hard. Saw a number of mountain lion tracks; also much beaver sign on Timothy Creek. Distance, about 10 miles. Privates Edwards and Rompre remained in camp. Mild; snowing all day.

February 19.—Following to head of Timothy and down Pelican Creek about 4 miles; thence across to Broad Creek, up it to hot springs near Fern Lake, arriving there about noon. Leaving Corporal Ornes to make camp, Corporal Herb and myself left for Ponuntpa Springs to look for buffalo. Found numerous signs of buffalo all around the spring and on both sides of Sour Creek. Followed them down Sour Creek to where a hot creek came down from a hot mountain on the north side, which they went up, and a close examination of the trail which they made going west to Hot Creek (the trail was not made in single file, but band was spread out). I estimated the band as follows: 4 calves, 8 bulls, about 8 or 9 cows, but think some of the signs which I took for cow signs may have been made by two-year-old bulls; in all 21 head. Ponuntpa Springs is an ideal wintering place for the band which is there, as there is no snow to speak of on the flat, which is about a mile long and three-fourths wide, and is covered with hot springs and hot creeks. The snow on Mirror Plateau is about 5 feet. Mild and fair weather. Distance, about 12 miles.

February 20.—Returned to camp on East Fork as went up. Temperature, mild; weather, fair. Distance, 18 miles.

February 21.—Entire party with pack train left for station (Soda Butte). Saw a few elk, also numerous signs of lynx on Cache Creek and Calfee Creek. Distance, 13 miles. Weather, stormy; temperature, mild.

February 22.—Left Soda Butte for Yancey's on return to post. Saw about 1,000 elk. Weather, fair; temperature, mild.

February 23.—Left Yancey's for post. Saw about 450 elk. Weather, fair; temperature, mild. All the game seen on this trip was in excellent condition for this time of the year.

February 25.—Scout Whittaker and myself left the post to patrol north line and locate Brundage's camp, and see if he had elk meat in his possession. Found that he had left his camp, but could not locate him. Saw about 400 antelope on flat in front of Gardiner; 3 blacktail deer on road to same place. Went from Gardiner to Brundage's camp on Eagle Creek, from there down Trail Creek to Horr, up Yellowstone River to Cinnabar, and thence by road to post. On the head of Trail Creek we saw James Forsyth and Frank Bezere with a wagon load of elk meat; followed the back trail, and found where they were killing, on Eagle Mountain, about 1¼ miles northwest of Gardiner. Weather, clear; temperature, mild. Distance, 25 miles.

February 26.—Scout Whittaker and myself left post to scout north line and meet train at Cinnabar. Saw 6 blacktail deer, 18 whitetail deer, about 400 antelope, and 4 elk. Weather, clear; temperature, mild. Distance, 17 miles.

[Scout Whittaker, 1898.]

February 23.—Left post with Private Martin and 2 pack mules, with grain for camp on McMahon Creek. After proceeding about 1 mile north of post I distinctly heard two shots fired near the north point of Sepulchre Mountain. I sent Private Martin on to camp, while I returned to post to inform Captain Erwin of the shooting I heard. Two men were detailed at once to go with me and see what had been done, or if anything had been killed. I took Sergeant Alexander and Private Lefler, of D Troop, and proceeded to the Government garden, where I met Sergeant Wall and Private Slough. I sent Sergeant Wall with Sergeant Alexander and Private Lefler and told him to put them on a hill above the Government Ice Lake, then come down where I was going to stop. I took Private Slough and patrolled along north line of the park to Gassert Creek, where I found the trail of a horse leading into the park; followed it, and saw where a man had dismounted from his horse and walked around awhile, then mounted his horse again and rode towards Cinnabar. I stayed out until 10 p. m., then returned to Sergeant Wall's camp. Sergeant Alexander returned to the post about 7.30 p. m. Saw about 300 elk near north point of Sepulchre Mountain; about 50 antelope on the Gardiner Flat. Weather, clear and warm.

February 24.—After packing up the mules I sent Private Martin to the post with them, while I took Private Slough and Sergeant Wall and patrolled the north line to Reese Creek. When I got to Cinnabar I was informed that Brundage was coming into Horr with a load of elk meat. Not knowing just what to do I sent Private Slough to the post with a letter to Captain Erwin for orders in this matter. About 7 p. m. I met Scout Morrison and Private Slough with orders from Captain Erwin to watch for Brundage and see if he had any meat in his possession. I sent Scout Morrison and Sergeant Wall to Trail Creek, while I watched the bridge at Gardiner. We stayed out until about 11 o'clock, but saw nothing of Brundage, and decided to return to the post. We arrived at the post about 12.30 p. m. Saw 14 elk back of Gassert ranch. Weather, clear and warm.

February 25.—Left post with Scout Morrison to make a trip to Eagle Creek and see if we could locate a band of 21 sheep, which were reported to have left the park. We saw nothing of them, but about 1 o'clock p. m. we came onto two men, Frank Bezere and James Forsyth, with a wagonload of elk meat, which had evidently just been killed. Frank Bezere asked us not to put him on the road for having the meat in his possession. We did not say anything, but went to Trail Creek, then to Horr, where we wired Captain Erwin about the meat we had seen. Then we proceeded to the post. Saw about 400 antelope at Gardiner, inside the park. Saw 6 deer near the post and 11 near the Government ice lake. Weather, clear and warm.

February 26.—Left post with Scout Morrison to patrol north line as far as Reese Creek. Went to Cinnabar. When train arrived, met Game Warden James F. Keown, who came up to arrest Bezere and Forsyth. He went to post to remain over night. We returned to post about 5 p. m. Saw about 350 antelope near Gardiner. Weather, clear and warm.

February 27.—Scout Morrison, State Game Warden James F. Keown, Sergeant Wall, Private Rompre, and myself left Fort Yellowstone to look for A. K. Crawford's camp and anybody that was violating the game laws. Mr. Keown and Scout Morrison went to Eagle Creek, while I took Private Rompre and Sergeant Wall and went down to Cedar Creek; scouted around there until about 4 p. m., then went to Cinnabar and remained over night. Mr. Keown and Scout Morrison returned to post. Saw 6 deer near the Government ice house; one had its front leg broken; I presume it was done while running. Weather, cloudy and warm.

February 28.—Received orders from Scout Morrison to meet himself and Mr. Keown at Gardiner with buckboard. We met there at about 9.30 a. m. After I saw Mr. Keown I told him I thought I could get him another case on Reese Creek if he could get along without me. He told me to go by all means and try to catch whoever was doing hunting at that place. I left Sergeant Wall and Private Rompre in his charge. After I got to Reese Creek I found the footprints of two men leading into the park, but could not find where they had done anything. I followed the tracks until about 3.30 p. m., when I saw the two men following a lot of elk trails that were there. I asked them if there was any game there. They said "Yes," but they could not find it. I started to go home, and after I went about 400 yards they started to follow me out. I suppose they were going back to the coal banks where they were from. I returned to the post about 5.30 p. m., and reported all the doings of my trip to Captain Erwin. Weather, cloudy and warm.

March 1.—Remained at post. Weather, cloudy and warm.

March 2.—Received orders to go to Livingston with Scout Morrison, in response to a telegram from State game warden to Captain Erwin, the acting superintendent of the park, to give our testimony in the Frank Bezere elk-killing case, which case was set for 6 o'clock p. m. On our testimony the accused was held for next term of district court. Said court convenes some time in the mouth of April. Weather, clear and warm.

March 3.—Returned from Livingston to Fort Yellowstone with Scout Morrison and reported for duty. Weather, cloudy and cold.

March 4.—Reported to Captain Erwin, the acting superintendent of the park, at 9 a. m., and received orders to take two men and eight days rations and work in the Reese Creek district, and as far east as the Gardiner River. At about 2 p. m. left post with Privates Rompre and Martin of H Troop, and Private Slough of D Troop, and four pack mules. Proceeded about 7 miles north of post and pitched camp at the north point of Sepulchre Mountain. After making camp I sent Private Martin back to post with all the mules. Saw about 250 antelope near Gardiner City; also saw a herd of 11 horses about 1 mile south of north line. Weather, cloudy and stormy.

March 5.—Left camp with Privates Rompre and Slough and patrolled the north line as far as the Gassert ranch; then I sent Privates Slough and Rompre back to camp, via Cinnabar, with orders to come to Reese Creek if I did not return to camp by 4 p. m. After leaving them I went to the McMahon ranch, on Reese Creek, to see if anybody was up there hunting, but learned that nobody had gone up there since last Tuesday. On that day two men brought out 1 elk, could not tell just where it was killed or who the men were, but they belonged in Horr. Saw about 75 antelope between Gardiner and Chadbourne's ranch, just outside the park, but they came back in the park towards evening. Saw 1 large bull elk near our camp. Weather, clear and very warm.

March 6.—Left camp with Private Rompre to patrol the north line as far as Reese Creek, and stayed there until 8.30 p. m., then returned to camp. Sent Private Slough to patrol east as far as the Gardiner River. He saw about 200 antelope near Gardiner, but inside the park. I saw about 50 near the Chadbourne ranch, outside the park, but they returned toward evening. There has been nobody on Reese Creek since Thursday night. The snow is going very fast on this creek. Weather, clear and very warm.

March 7.—Left camp with Privates Rompre and Slough to round up a herd of 9 horses that have been running on the park and send them into the post. After I got them started I let Privates Rompre and Slough take them to the post, while I patrolled the north line to Reese Creek again. After I got to Reese Creek I went down to Horr to see if I could find out anything about "Scotty" Crawford or Brundage, but I did not succeed in getting any information of Brundage. But "Scotty" was in Horr last night; I was told that he had given up hunting for meat. I went back to Reese Creek and remained there until 5.30 p. m., when it began raining so hard that I decided to return to camp, there being no sign of anybody up there to-day. Privates Slough and Rompre report seeing about 250 antelope near Government ice lake; they saw 8 deer near our camp. I saw 13 back of the Gassert ranch—all blacktail. They must have just moved in there; it is the first time I have seen them there this winter. Weather, cloudy and warm; wind blowing and raining in afternoon.

March 8.—Left camp with Private Slough and patrolled along the line to the Gardiner River, thence back to camp. Remained in camp until about 6.30 p. m., then started down to lay at Reese Creek. When I got there found out that there had been nobody up there, yet I returned to camp about 11 p. m. While in Gardiner learned that Brundage had been there yesterday, but did not bring in any meat. He returned to his camp last night. I saw about 350 antelope near Gardiner, but inside the park. I saw about 50 last night when I was coming back to camp from Reese Creek, along the road between Gardiner and Cinnabar, just above the Chadbourne ranch, but nothing seems to molest them. About 2 inches of snow fell here last night. Weather, cloudy; cold wind blowing all day

March 9.—Left camp with Private Rompre to make a patrol to Reese Creek. I sent Private Slough to patrol to McMahon Creek, on Mount Evarts. When I got to Cinnabar I wrote Captain Erwin, the acting superintendent of the park, a letter requesting that I be allowed to remain in camp until Sunday night; also wrote a letter in regard to "Scotty" Crawford, but later I learned the information was false and wired the same to Captain Erwin. Towards evening I went to Horr. I remained there until 5 30 p. m., then went up to Reese Creek. There was nobody up there. I layed along the Yellowstone River until about 7.30 p. m., then I went to Cinnabar and remained there until 9 p. m., then returned to camp. While at Horr learned that Brundage had a contract to furnish elk meat to a certain party, for a debt he owes to said party, to the amount of 1,500 pounds. Also saw two men come in with guns and a rope which had blood on it. Don't know where they came from. Saw about 75 antelope near Gardiner, inside the park, 12 deer back of Gassert ranch. Private Slough saw about 100 antelope on the McMahon bench at north point of Mount Evarts. A. K. Crawford went up to Bear Gulch to-day. Weather, cloudy and cold; wind blowing.

March 10.—Sent Private Slough to Reese Creek while I took Private Rompre and went to the post to report to Captain Erwin and see if I could return to camp and remain until Sunday. My request was granted, and I took two days' rations and Private Martin, with one pack mule, and returned to camp at 5 o'clock p. m. Sent Private Martin back to post with the mule. I saw about 100 antelope near Gardiner, about 100 on Mount Evarts, 2 deer on Mount Evarts, 6 on the Government dump, 9 near the Government ice lake, all blacktails. Saw 10 mountain sheep on Mount Evarts, near McMahon coal bank. Weather, cloudy and cold; wind blowing. About 6.30 p. m. Private Slough and myself met "Scotty" Crawford's partner going towards Gardiner with one pack horse loaded with grub. He went up to Bear Gulch.

March 11.—Sent Privates Rompre and Slough to Reese Creek while I made a patrol to the Gardiner River, thence back to camp. I saw nothing on my trip, but Rompre reported seeing 1 large bull elk on Reese Creek with one hind leg broken. About 4 p. m. decided to go to the post and ask Captain Erwin to let Scout Morrison come down to-morrow and go with me to Eagle Creek and see where "Scotty" Crawford's partner had gone to. I left the post again at 7.15 p. m., and patroled the road back as far as Chadbourne's ranch, then returned to camp. I saw 15 black-tail deer on river bed, just opposite the Boiling River, 9 white-tail deer near the Government ice house, 57 antelope on west slope of Mount Evarts, just opposite the Boiling River. Captain Erwin told me he would have Scout Morrison meet me to-morrow. Weather, stormy and cold.

March 12.—Sent Private Slough to make a patrol to Gardiner River, then return to camp. After he had returned to camp I sent him with Private Rompre to make a patrol to Reese Creek again, while I went to meet Scout Morrison. I met Scout Morrison about 10 a. m., and proceeded to Eagle Creek; saw nothing there and returned to camp. There I found Privates Rompre and Slough in camp; they reported nothing on Reese Creek. Scout Morrison and myself saw George Mack, of Gardiner, hunting along the north line of the park, about 500 yards west of Gardiner. When he saw us, he came back to the road again and back to Gardiner. We saw about 75 antelope on the east side of Gardiner River, on the Gardiner Flat. Scout Morrison said he saw a great many in the J. C. McCartney field. The 13 deer that were back of the Gassert ranch have moved back into the park and up near the ice lake. Weather, cloudy; temperature, mild.

March 13.—Started out from camp on foot with Private Rompre to watch a small band of antelope near the north line, about 400 yards west of Gardiner. I saw two men near the line. Both of them had guns and were evidently hunting. I watched them until they returned to Gardiner. One of them fired two shots, but I could not see where he had killed anything. One of them was George Mack, of Gardiner. I returned to camp about 12.30 p. m., and found Private Martin had just arrived with the pack mules. I packed them up and sent him back to the post with Private Slough about 1.30 p. m., then took Private Rompre and went to Reese Creek. There had been nobody up there since I made camp here. I returned to the post about 7.30 p. m., and reported everything to First Lieut. G. O. Cress, the commanding officer. I saw about 300 antelope near the road about 400 yards west of Gardiner and outside the park. I reported the fact to Lieutenant Cress, who detailed 2 men to patrol the line to-morrow morning. Also saw about 150 on east side of the Gardiner Flat. Weather, very cold and stormy. About 4 inches of snow fell in our camp last night and to-day.

March 14.—Left the post with Lieutenant Arnold and 17 privates to shovel out the Golden Gate. Did not have much trouble in getting to the Gate, and it only took about three hours to get through the Gate. For about one-half mile from the Glen Creek Bridge we had to shovel a great deal of snow. Then it was easy to get to the Klamer cabin. From there on saw about 100 elk in the vicinity of Swan Lake Flat. Weather, stormy and cold.

March 15.—Left post and went to Gardiner and overtook 2 men who were sent out early in the morning. I took Private Hoover and sent Private Newman to post; then went along the line to Reese Creek, then came back to Cinnabar; stayed there until about 5 p. m., then started for the post. Saw about 300 antelope near Gardiner inside the park. In the evening saw about 75 near the road outside the park. Saw 17 blacktail deer, 4 in Government garden, 14 near Boiling River. Weather, cloudy and cold; wind blowing.

March 16.—Left the post with First Lieut. G. O. Cress, the commanding officer, and rode up to the McMahon ranche, on north point of Mount Evarts; thence over to Gardiner Flat, then over to the J. C. McCartney field, then to the post via Government garden. Saw 1 blacktail deer near the Government ice house, 1 whitetail deer at the crossing of the old road over the Gardiner River, about 25 antelope on the west slope of Mount Evarts, almost opposite the Boiling River, and between 150 and 175 in the vicinity of Gardiner Flats and about 50 near the J. C. McCartney field. Saw 8 mountain sheep on the bluff near the Eagle's Nest, 5 deer on the west slope of Mount Evarts, opposite the first bridge over the Gardiner River from post. Weather clear and warm. At the Government garden we saw a duck going down the river on its back, and landed on the opposite side of the river. I then went over and caught it and found it bleeding from the head. Saw some fresh beaver sign just below the first bridge over the Gardiner River north of the post.

March 17.—Left the post with Lieutenant Hawkins to make a patrol to Reese Creek, then back to the post. Saw about 150 antelope in the vicinity of Gardiner Flat and north point of Mount Evarts, and about 150 west of Gardiner, some outside the park and some inside. Saw 10 mountain sheep on Mount Evarts, 24 elk near Government ice lake. Mr. McMahon informed us that some meat had been taken out yesterday. Weather, clear in the a. m. and cloudy in the p. m.

March 18.—Remained in post. Weather cloudy.

March 19.—Left the post with Sergeant Alexander, of D Troop, and Private Boniface, of H Troop; proceeded 7 miles north of the post and went into camp in my old camp at the north point of Sepulchre Mountain for three days. Saw about 50 antelope above the Boiling River on the east side of the Gardiner River, 29 near the first bridge over the Gardiner River north of the post, 11 blacktail deer about the same place, 2 at the Government garden, 9 near the Government ice lake. Arrived in camp about 7.30 p. m. Weather, stormy and cold.

March 20.—In the morning I took Sergeant Alexander and went on top of a high hill so we could see everything that took place on the north line of the park, between Gardiner and Reese Creek. We saw nothing up to 12.30 o'clock p. m. and returned to camp and left for Reese Creek about 5.30 p. m. There had been nothing up there since my last trip, which was on the 17th instant. We saw 8 deer near the Gassert ranche. Saw about 50 antelope one-half mile west of Gardiner and about 500 yards north of the park line. We returned to camp about 8.30 p. m. Weather, cloudy and cold; wind blowing.

March 21.—Left camp on foot with Sergeant Alexander and went almost to the park line to look for the antelope, but owing to the inclement weather we could do nothing, so we returned to camp until about 4.30 p. m. We then took our horses and rode along the park line as far west as the Gassert ranch, but saw nothing, so we returned to camp. It was almost impossible to do anything on account of the intense cold. We saw 3 blacktail deer about 300 yards north of our camp; 10 elk about 700 yards east of camp; all inside the park. Weather, stormy and very cold.

March 22.—Left camp with Sergeant Alexander and patrolled the north line as far as Reese Creek, thence back to camp. We left camp about 3.30 p. m. and went to Fort Yellowstone. Saw nothing on Reese Creek. Game seen to-day, about 150 antelope about 400 yards north of the park line and about one-half mile west of Gardiner; 3 blacktail deer one-fourth mile north of our camp; 19 blacktail deer near the McMahon coal bank on north point of Mount Evarts; 6 near the Government ice house one-fourth mile north of the post; 25 elk about one-half mile east of our camp; about 300 elk on Mount Evarts near the McMahon coal bank. Arrived at post 6.30 p. m. Weather, clear; very cold at night and warm during the day.

March 23.—Left the post with Private Murphy, of D Troop, on snowshoes and went around Mount Evarts down Rescue Creek to Blacktail, thence back to post. Saw about 125 elk on east end of Mount Evarts; 6 mountain sheep same place. Weather, cloudy and cold.

March 24.—Left the post, mounted, about 10 a. m. to make patrol to Reese Creek, then back to post. Saw 3 men near the outlet of Gardiner River; think they were fishing, but could not swear to it. Saw about 125 antelope in the vicinity of Gardiner Flat; 52 on east side of Gardiner River, opposite Boiling River; 23 blacktail deer same place; also 8 near McMahon ranch on Reese Creek. Saw 14 mountain sheep on top of bluff at Eagle's Nest—7 ewes and 1 ram in one bunch and 6 ewes in the other. Saw about 300 elk near the head of McMahon Creek. Weather, clear and chinook wind blowing.

March 25.—Left post, mounted, with Private Palmer, of H Troop, to make patrol along north line to Reese Creek, thence back to the post. Left post 10.20 a. m., returned 4.10 p. m. Saw about 75 antelope on Gardiner Flat; 6 blacktail deer about 300 yards east of the post sawmill. Went to Reese Creek, but saw nothing there; the weather was too stormy to see very far off. Weather, stormy; light snow falling all day but not very cold.

March 26.—Left the post with Private Bledsoe, of D Troop. Went to the outlet of Gardiner River, then west along the park line to Reese Creek. At Gardiner I found a fresh foot track leading into the park; followed it and found it to be Thomas Newcomb, but he had no arms with him. On the road to Gardiner I saw 4 mountain sheep at the Eagle's Nest. Saw about 75 antelope on the Gardiner Flat; about 150 400 yards west of Gardiner but inside the park; 13 blacktail deer near the Government ice house; 4 at the Government garden. Weather, stormy and cold.

March 27.—Remained in the post. Weather, clear; temperature, cold.

March 28.—Left the post to patrol to Reese Creek, but before I reached there I came across 2 footprints of men going towards the park and I decided to come up Reese Creek, then go back and follow the tracks. There was nobody on Reese Creek to-day. On my return I took up the trail of the 2 men. Had some difficulty in finding it once in a while, but I finally struck it where the snow was deep and found that there were 3 men instead of 2, and that they had gone about one-half mile into the park and there shot and killed 1 cow elk, and it looked as if they had wounded 2 others. They took the meat out last night. There were tracks of 2 men hunting along the line, but they did not get inside the park. I saw 7 mountain sheep at Eagle's Nest; 37 antelope on the west side of Gardiner River; about 75 at the junction of the Gardiner and Yellowstone rivers; about 250 1 mile west of Gardiner, and about 300 yards north of the park line saw 35 blacktail deer, between the Government ice lake and Gardiner River; 4 near the Eagle's Nest; 4 at the two-mile post north of the post; 6 whitetail at the Boiling River; 5 in the Government garden. Weather, clear; temperature, mild.

March 29.—Left the post with Lieutenant Lindsley; went to Gardiner City, then to Cinnabar, then to Horr, then back to where the elk were killed yesterday, then back to the post. Saw 42 elk on the north slope of Sepulchre Mountain, about 15 near the Gardiner ice lake; 3 blacktail deer near the Government garden; about 50 antelope on the Gardiner Flat on the north point of Mount Evarts. Weather, clear in the forenoon, cloudy in the afternoon; temperature, mild.

March 30.—Left the post with Scout Morrison, on skis, and proceeded to Norris. Saw no game. At Willow Park we met Corporal Moore, Private Root, and Private Fremont coming in off pass. Weather, cloudy; temperature, mild.

March 31 (12 miles).—Left Norris with Scout Morrison and proceeded to Canyon Hotel. Saw no game on trip to-day. Weather, clear; temperature, mild.

April 1.—Left Canyon Hotel with Scout Morrison and proceeded to Lake Hotel. We took lunch at Mud Geyser Station. Took Privates Price and Canivan with us from there to Lake Hotel, intending to take them to the Thumb; but when we arrived at the Lake we found Sergeant Leob and two privates from Snake River Station. Scout Morrison and myself then decided to make up our trips from here. I am to take Privates Price and Canivan from Mud Geyser and Private Montgomery of Snake River Station, and go up the Upper Yellowstone River, then to Snake River Station, while he would take Sergeant Leob and Private Carter, and we would meet at that place. Saw 2 foxes and 1 coyote in Hayden Valley. Weather, clear; temperature, mild.

April 2.—Left Lake Hotel with Private Montgomery, of the Snake River Station, Privates Canivan and Price, of Mud Geyser Station, and proceeded to Beaverdam Creek. We went from Lake Hotel straight across the Yellowstone Lake to the lean-to on Beaverdam. The lean-to is filled up with gravel and snow so we could not stay in it, but had to camp in the woods near by. At Terrace Point we saw 14 elk and numerous signs of others. Saw 5 dead elk—last spring calves. Saw what I took to be two moose tracks near the east end of the lake on the mouth of Beaverdam Creek. Saw one fresh bear track which was made to-day along Beaverdam Creek. Have seen no signs of beaver at this place yet. Saw no signs of any poaching having been done. Will venture to say there are between 150 and 200 elk between Terrace Point and Beaverdam Creek. Weather, clear; temperature, warm.

April 3.—Same party left Beaverdam Creek and proceeded to the old Crawford cabin near Atlantic Creek. Camped there over night. There was a lynx at the cabin which had killed something and dragged it to the cabin. I think he had killed a lot of jack rabbits or else another lynx and eaten it up there at the cabin. There has been nobody at the cabin since the rations were put there, nor has there been any poaching done in that district this winter. At least there are no signs of any having been done. Saw 13 bull elk near the outlet of Mountain Creek; also saw signs of 6 moose between Beaverdam Creek and Mountain Creek. The Upper Yellowstone River is open in some places. From Mountain Creek to Crawford cabin there is no sign of game of any kind. The snow is too deep to permit any animal to live in it. Weather, clear and warm. Twenty miles.

April 4.—The same party left Crawford Cabin and proceeded to the gold mines on Pacific Creek. Went up Atlantic Creek and down Pacific Creek. We saw no sign of any game until we got to Coral Creek; there we saw one fresh bear track. The snow will average 7 or 8 feet in depth in that country. Weather, clear; temperature, hot. Twenty-one miles.

YELLOWSTONE NATIONAL PARK. 79

April 5.—Same party left gold mines on Pacific Creek and proceeded to Snake River Station. Saw no game of any kind. Left gold mines at 8 a. m.; arrived at station at 7.30 p. m. All the game I have seen is in very good condition; I don't think they will have any trouble in getting through the rest of the winter. Weather, clear and warm.

April 6.—Same party remained at the Snake River Station to wait for Scout Morrison and party to return from the Falls River country. Weather, clear and warm, but very stormy towards evening.

April 7.—Party still remaining at station, waiting for Scout Morrison and party. Scout Morrison and party returned from Falls River country to-day. Weather, very stormy, but not cold.

April 8.—Remained at Snake River Station. Weather, cloudy; temperature, warm.

April 9.—Left Snake River Station with Scout Morrison, Sergeant Leob and Private Carter of Snake River Station, and Privates Canivan and Price of Mud Geyser Station, and proceeded to Shoshone Geyser Basin. Camped near the Union Geyser. Saw signs of 6 or 7 elk on Polecat Creek. Weather, clear; temperature, warm. Thirty miles.

April 10.—Same party left Shoshone Geyser Basin and proceeded to Upper Geyser Basin lunch station via Lone Star Geyser. Left camp 4.40 a. m.; arrived Upper Basin 8.30 a. m. Saw no sign of any large game. Saw no sign of anybody having been in that country this winter. Saw one pine marten at Upper Basin. Weather, cloudy; temperature, warm.

April 11.—Same party left Upper Geyser Basin and proceeded to Lower Geyser Basin or Fountain Hotel. Five miles from Upper Basin, on the road to the Fountain Hotel, we saw a trail across the road, and, to the best of my knowledge, it was a trail made by buffalo, but could not tell how many of them had made the trail, it being about three or four days old. I think they were going north; there were at least 3 of them on the trail. Toward Mary's Mountain there are a great many elk signs between the Excelsior Geyser and the Fountain Station. There is a great deal of bare ground between the Upper and Lower Basins and snow is very soft. We had to wade about one-half of the way. We went to the station and remained over night with Corporal Holman. Weather, clear; temperature, mild. Ten miles.

April 12.—Left Fountain Station with Scout Morrison, Sergeant Leob, and Private Carter of Snake River, and proceeded to Norris Station. Stayed there over night. There is about 6 miles of bare ground between Fountain and Norris Basin. Saw a few elk sign in Gibbon Canyon. Privates Canivan and Price left me at Fountain Station to go back to their station at Mud Geyser; they will go over Mary's Mountain and through the Hayden Valley. We arrived at Norris about 8.30 a. m. Weather, clear; temperature, warm. Twenty miles.

April 13.—Same party left Norris and proceeded to Fort Yellowstone. Left Norris at 3 a. m.; arrived at post at 8.10 a. m. Saw no game on road. The snow is going very fast. This entire trip from March 30 to the present day has been made on skis and covers a distance of about 235 miles in all. All the game I have seen is in very good condition. The rations in the Beaverdam and Crawford cabins are in bad condition, except the coffee. The mice and rats have got into the boxes and have eaten up some of them, and what they did not eat they have spoiled. Private Price of the Mud Geyser Station is a very good man to have on such a trip. Private Montgomery went snow-blind at the Crawford cabin and could hardly get to Snake River Station. We had to walk into the post from Golden Gate. Weather, clear; temperature, warm. Twenty miles.

April 14.—Left the post with Scout Morrison, mounted and went to Cinnabar, then back to the post. Saw 36 blacktail deer near the Boiling River; 30 antelope—22 opposite the Boiling River, 8 on the Gardiner Flat. Saw a fire burning about 300 yards north of the park line near the Gardiner Ice Lake. Weather, clear and warm.

April 15.—Left post, mounted, and went around Mount Everts to try and locate the mountain sheep. Saw 7 near the coal bank, 4 on Turkey Pen, 4 on east end of Mount Everts. Saw 65 blacktail deer—7 about 200 yards east of post hospital, 4 on McMahon Creek, 10 on Turkey Pen road, 1 on Red Mountain, 10 on Cooke City road on East Gardiner River, 21 on west slope of Mount Everts, about 600 yards east of Boiling River, 12 opposite the Boiling River. Saw 67 antelope on Turkey Pen road, 27 near the coal banks, 19 opposite Boiling River; 5 bull elk at the top of the Gardiner grade. Weather, clear; temperature, hot.

April 16.—Left post, mounted, and went over old road to Reese Creek. Saw 11 mountain sheep on top of Mount Everts, about 150 antelope on the Gardiner Flat, 7 whitetail deer 1 mile west of Gardiner and about 300 yards north of park line. Weather, cloudy and rainy at Cinnabar; temperature, mild.

April 17.—Remained in post. Weather, cloudy; temperature, warm.

April 18.—Remained in post. Roached pack mules in the forenoon. Weather, clear and warm.

April 19.—Remained in the post. Weather, clear; temperature, warm.

April 20.—Went to Livingston, Mont., with Scout Morrison, on the case of Frank Bezere for killing elk, to give our testimony in said case. Weather, rainy; temperature, cold at Cinnabar.

April 21.—Attended court in Livingston, Mont., to give testimony against Frank Bezere, defendant; he was found "not guilty." Weather, cloudy; temperature, warm.

April 22.—Returned from Livingston, Mont., to Fort Yellowstone and reported for duty to the commanding officer. Arrived at post at 2.45 p. m. At 5.45 p. m., left post with Sergeant Welch and 2 pack mules and went to Gardiner to get some Tom Moore pack saddles; returned to post at 9 p. m. Saw 14 blacktail deer between Boiling River and the Government ice house. Saw 4 mountain sheep at Eagle's Nest, about 150 antelope on the Gardiner Flat. Weather, cloudy and rainy in Gardiner and Cinnabar; temperature, mild.

April 23.—Left the post, mounted, with Sergeant Welch, Private Hemstead and Private Holt of H Troop, and 4 pack mules and 2 lead horses, and proceeded to Norris Station. We left post at 9.45 a. m., arrived at Crystal Spring 1.15 p. m. Left Crystal Spring at 2.10 p. m., arrived at Norris 5 p. m. We made the trip in about six hours travel, which was remarkably good time, this being the first mounted party to make the trip this spring. There was about 5 miles of pretty deep snow, but it was so soft that a horse could pass right through it without much trouble; the rest was easy traveling. Private Helm met us at Bijah Spring. We saw several bear tracks on the road between Twin Lakes and Norris. Weather, clear; temperature, hot.

April 24.—Left Norris, mounted, with Private Hemstead and 2 pack mules and went to the Riverside Station. There was not a great deal of snow on the road in the 26 miles we traveled. We did not go through more than 4 miles of snow, and it was so soft that it was just like going through so much water. The ground is very soft in some places. There is some fallen timber and a great many rocks in the road in Gibbon Canyon; in fact, the road is in very bad condition for a team to get over them before they are repaired. Saw about 50 elk at the forks of the Gibbon and Firehole rivers, 3 fresh bear tracks in Gibbon Canyon, several in Madison Canyon. From Norris Sergeant Welch and Private Holt took 2 mules and returned to the post. I wired the Fountain men to meet me at the forks of the road and take their led horse to their place until I came back from Riverside. I met Corporal Holman in the Madison Canyon going to his station. Weather, clear; temperature, very hot, and does not freeze any at night.

April 25.—Left station with Sergeant Bernstein, mounted, and rode north to Maple Creek, then returned to station. Saw some fresh elk sign in the fallen timber close to Maple Creek. Sergeant Bernstein showed me where 3 elk were killed last December. They were inside the park about 8 miles north of the station, or 1 mile west of north. Sent Private Norvell and Private Will into the post from here, so that they would not have to go to the Fountain. Decided to hold Private Ornes and the mules over to-day; the stock was a little tired. There is no snow to speak of around here or Sand Butte, but the ground is very soft and a horse mires down very easy. It would be very hard for any poacher to get into the park just now. Weather, clear; temperature, hot.

April 26.—Left Riverside Station with Sergeant Bernstein, Private Ornes, and Private Hemstead, and went to Fountain Station. At the forks of the road, I sent Private Hemstead to Norris. Saw a great many fresh elk tracks in Gibbon Canyon. The roads are drying up very fast. There is no snow around this place. Weather, clear; temperature, hot; high wind blowing.

April 27.—When I got up this morning I found my horse and the 2 mules gone; began to look for them and found they had gone to Norris. I saddled up Private Ornes's horse and went after them. It was 11.30 a. m. before I got to Norris. I started back at 1 p. m.; arrived here at 5.10 p. m. I sent Privates Burdette and Stitham on their way to the post and told them to take Private Hemstead with them when they left Norris and I would take Private Ornes and go clear through to the post to-morrow with the pack mules. The wind storm of yesterday did a great deal of damage in the Gibbon Canyon to the telephone line. It is broken in about 25 places and down for about one-half mile in some places and there are at least 100 fallen trees across the road, and the most of them will have to be cut out before a wagon can get through. In my orders for this trip, I was ordered to take Corporal Holman from the Fountain and make a trip on skis up to Bear Parks, stay there over night, and next day go out as far as possible and return to cabin again. Not being able to make the trip at present on account of sickness, I decided to go to the post and report the fact to Lieutenant Lindsley. I could not get any message over the telephone because the wires were down. There has been a band of elk come up the road from the Madison Canyon to the Twin Buttes. There are about 500 elk in this vicinity. One fresh beaver sign in Nez Perce Creek about 2 miles above the station. Weather, clear; temperature, hot. Distance, 40 miles.

YELLOWSTONE NATIONAL PARK. 81

April 28.—Left station with Private Ornes and Private Sybert, mounted, with 2 mules and proceeded to Fort Yellowstone. Left Fountain at 7.30 a. m.; stopped at Norris for dinner; left Norris at 1.30 p. m. Saw where 2 elk crossed the road at Crystal Spring, 2 at Obsidian Cliff; several fresh beaver signs in the road between the Fountain and Crystal Spring; 4 Elk on Swan Lake flat. The telephone wire is down very badly all around the park. Very little snow between Norris and the post. Weather, cloudy; temperature, warm.

April 29.—Remained in the post. Weather, cloudy; temperature, mild.

April 30.—Remained in the post on account of sickness. Cloudy, snowing a little; temperature, cold.

May 1.—Remained in the post on account of sickness. Weather, cloudy; temperature, cold.

May 2.—Left post, mounted, with Scout Morrison and made patrol to J. S. Knowles' cabin on the Yellowstone River. Saw about 300 elk near Blacktail Creek; 8 blacktail deer near the outlet of the creek; 5 antelope same place. The beaver on Lava Creek are not working any this spring—at least there are no signs of any work. The beaver in Blacktail Creek are doing some great work at present. They are building some fine dams on the creek, about 1 mile from its outlet. Weather, cloudy; temperature, cold.

May 3.—Left J. S. Knowles's cabin with Scout Morrison and returned to the post. Saw some signs of people fishing on the Yellowstone River above Mr. Knowles' place. They come up from Gardiner and camp over night in an old cabin near Knowles' place and fish from there. We saw 1 man fishing on the river on the east side, opposite mouth of Blacktail Creek; his name was Mike O'Brien, from Gardiner City. Saw 3 dead elk, last spring calves, near the Blacktail ford. Saw about 200 elk on Blacktail; 2 antelope same place. I saw 2 and Morrison saw 6 mountain sheep near mouth of Blacktail. Weather, cloudy and cold.

May 4.—Remained in the post, owing to sickness. Weather, cloudy; temperature, cold.

May 5.—Left post with Scout Morrison, mounted, to make a patrol to headwaters of the Gardiner River and Indian Creek, but could not get there on account of deep snow. Saw about 30 elk near Mr. Klamer's slaughterhouse on Swan Lake Flat. Weather, cloudy; temperature, cool.

May 6.—Left post, mounted, with Scout Morrison and 2 pack mules to make patrol to Hellroaring Creek. Camped at the mouth of Cottonwood Creek. Saw 2 men fishing on the Yellowstone River; they had about 30 pounds of fish between them. Saw quite a number of elk in the vicinity of Blacktail Creek. Saw 10 blacktail deer on the Cooke City road along the Gardiner grade. Met Lieutenant Lindsley with pack train at Blacktail Creek on his return to post from Soda Butte Station. Weather, cloudy; temperature, mild.

May 7.—Left camp on Cottonwood Creek and rode over to Hellroaring Creek. Saw 4 whitetail deer and 4 blacktail between Cottonwood and Hellroaring creeks. Found 2 dead bull elks that died this spring, and 7 that I believe were killed for their teeth alone; but they were killed last year if they were killed at all. Weather, clear; temperature, mild.

May 8.—Left camp and returned to the post. Saw about 25 elk on Blacktail Creek; 1 antelope same place; 10 blacktail deer on the Gardiner grade on Cooke City road. The Yellowstone River is very high at present; will be hard to ford from now on. Weather, clear; temperature, warm.

May 9.—Left post, mounted, and went to Gardiner City to get some pack saddles. Returned to post at 7 p. m. Saw 11 mountain sheep on Mount Evarts, opposite Boiling River; 1 at the Eagle's Nest. Weather, clear; temperature, warm.

May 10.—Remained in the post to fix up the pack-train outfit for use. Weather, cloudy; temperature, warm.

May 11.—Remained in the post to work on the pack train. Weather, clear; temperature, warm.

May 12.—Remained in the post on account of sickness. Weather, clear; temperature, warm.

May 13.—Left the post with Mr. A. E. Burns to make patrol on Reese Creek. Mr. McMahon informed me that A. K. Crawford was up on Reese Creek last Sunday. We followed up the creek and saw where somebody had gone up into the park, but they came out again. I presume they were trying to get into the park. We saw 5 deer near the Boiling River. Weather, clear; temperature, warm.

May 14.—Left post, mounted, with A. E. Burns and 1 pack mule, and proceeded to the headwaters of Glen Creek; camped there over night. Saw 6 elk on the west slope of Sepulchre Mountain. Weather, clear; temperature, warm.

May 15.—Left camp on Glen Creek, and went to head of Reese Creek, down said creek to the McMahon ranch, then to the Gassert ranch, then along the foot of Sepulchre Mountain to the post. Saw 13 deer at the old brickyard on the old Gardiner road, 3 near the Transportation barn. Weather, cloudy; hard rain falling around

Electric Peak. There are quite a number of bear signs and fresh elk signs also. There are about 25 head of cattle and a few horses running on the park southwest of Gardiner City. There has been nobody through the Electric Peak Pass yet, but there are some fresh horse tracks along the park line on Reese Creek.

May 16.—Remained in the post on account of sickness. Weather, cloudy and rainy; temperature, cool.

May 17.—Went to Gardiner and returned to the post; saw 3 deer near the old brickyard; intended to start for Yancey's in the afternoon, but the weather was bad, so received orders to wait until morning. Weather, cloudy and rainy; temperature, mild.

May 18.—Left post with A. E. Burns, mounted, and 3 pack mules, and proceeded to Yancey's Hotel; saw 2 deer on the new Cooke City road, 4 near the halfway place, 4 in the Devils Gut, 4 antelope near the Blacktail Creek; also a great many elk scattered along the road to Yancey's—at least 400 of them. The beaver in the Blacktail Creek have not been molested this spring and they are doing a great deal of work all along the creek. In the vicinity of Yancey's place the beaver are increasing very rapidly; all the small creeks have beaver in them now; they are doing a great deal of work at present and have not been molested by anyone. Weather, cloudy and rainy; temperature, mild.

May 19.—Remained at Yancey's owing to the inclement weather; also to prospect the beaver dams in all the creeks around here; found them all in good condition and beaver doing a great deal of work on them; saw 25 elk near the hot spring, 2 miles southeast of Yancey's. Weather, cloudy; drizzling rain all day; temperature, mild.

May 20.—Left Yancey's and proceeded to Soda Butte; saw about 3,000 elk between Yancey's and Soda Butte, 37 antelope between Junction Butte and Little Specimen Creek, 17 deer near the Junction Butte. The beaver are doing a great deal of work in the streams around this district. Weather, cloudy and very stormy; temperature, cold.

May 21.—I remained at the station while Burns went up to Death Gulch and Cache Creek. Private Edwards went to Hellroaring Creek; Herb went with Burns. Privates Root, McDonald, and Palmer arrived to-day to relieve the present detachment. Herb and Burns report 11 dead bear in Death Gulch. Weather, cloudy; temperature, mild.

May 22.—Left station with A. E. Burns and went to J. S. Knowles' cabin on Crevasse Creek. Private Hardin and Private McDonald left station ahead of me to meet Private Edwards on Slough Creek; we met them all at that place. Slough Creek and Hellroaring Creek are up pretty high, but we had no difficulty in crossing them. On our way down the river I saw a man fishing along the bank, about 150 yards above the ford; did not say anything to him, but came down to the old cabin below Knowles' place, and there I found a man camped. I asked him what he was doing and he said himself and 2 other men were fishing. I went into the cabin and found about 20 pounds of fish hanging up in a secluded place. Everything looked rather suspicious to me; the man at the cabin said the other two were out fishing; but I saw 2 poles and 2 sacks at the cabin, and I concluded he was not telling the truth about the matter. I had come down the river myself and saw but one man, while the other ones were not there, as he had told me. They had been here three days—two of them—while the third one had come up last night. I told them they would have to stop fishing and return to Gardiner. They leave to-morrow morning. Saw about 2,500 elk between Soda Butte and Cotton Creek; 2 deer and 7 antelope on Slough Creek. Weather, cloudy; hard rain in the evening; temperature, mild.

May 23.—Left camp at J. S. Knowles', and proceeded to Fort Yellowstone. Before leaving camp, I went down to see if the 3 men who were fishing had left their cabin; found they had gone. When we went through Gardiner, I saw them there. Saw no game. Weather, cloudy and raining hard part of the day; temperature, cold.

May 24.—Remained in the post until 3 p. m., then took Private Kelner and 1 pack mule and went to J. S. Knowles' cabin on Crevasse Creek with order from the commanding officer and Acting Superintendent of the park to destroy all the cabins around Knowles' place. I burned 4 of them; 1 belonged to Tom Miner, 1 to Charles White, 1 to David Borem, and 1 to J. S. Knowles. I moved everything out before setting them on fire. Saw quite a number of grouse on Crevasse Mountain. John Ballinger is camped about one-half mile from the park line; saw where he had been in the park on foot on Crevasse Mountain. Weather, cloudy; temperature, cool.

May 25.—Left Knowles' to return to the post. Before leaving I looked at all the cabins that had been burned to see that there was no danger of fire spreading; found them all about out. The Yellowstone River is very high and muddy. Saw 1 deer, 1 mile north of the post. Weather, cloudy; temperature, cool.

May 26.—Left post and went to H. E. Klamer's slaughterhouse and stayed there over night. Weather, cloudy; temperature, cold.

May 27.—Left slaughterhouse and rode up almost to the pocket on Fawn Creek.

The beaver have not done any work on this creek this spring. Three dams have been torn out, but it has been done a year or two ago. Saw about 300 elk on Fawn Creek and 27 on the Gardiner River. The beaver in Gardiner River are doing some work; but, owing to the high water, it is hard to tell how many there are in the district. Weather, clear; temperature, mild.

May 28.—Left post with Private Williams, of D Troop, and returned to the Gardiner River, then up Indian Creek to the foot of Bighorn Pass. The beaver are doing some work at present and have not been molested this spring, or up to the present time. There are about 500 elk near the headwaters of Indian Creek, 57 on Panther Creek, and 7 on Gardiner River. Left post at 7.45 a. m., returned at 3.30 p. m. Weather, cloudy; raining part of the day, and very cold.

May 29.—Remained in the post. Weather, cloudy; temperature, cool.

May 30.—Left post and went to Gardiner and Cinnabar. Returned to post this afternoon; went down to gather information. Weather, cloudy, stormy, and cold.

May 31.—Owing to no appropriation being made, I was laid off; this is the end of my scouting duty.

[James G. Morrison.]

March 26, 1898.—Remained at post. Weather, stormy; temperature, mild.
March 27.—Remained at post. Weather, clear; temperature, cold.
March 28.—Remained at post. Weather, clear; temperature, mild.
March 29.—Remained at post. Weather, clear; temperature, mild.
March 30.—Scout Whittaker and myself left post for Snake River Station. Stopped at Norris over night. Weather, cloudy; temperature, mild.
March 31.—Left Norris for Canyon. Weather, clear; temperature, mild.
April 1.—Went to the lake from Canyon, stopping at Mud Geyser for luncheon, and taking Privates Price and Canivan with us. Met Sergeant Leob, Privates Carter and Montgomery, from Snake River, at lake. Saw about 50 swan, 4 foxes, 2 coyotes. Weather, clear; temperature, mild. Distance, 17 miles.
April 2.—Scout Whittaker, Privates Canivan, Price, and Montgomery left Lake Hotel for Beaverdam cabin. Myself, Sergeant Leob, and Private Carter left Lake Hotel for Snake River Station; stopped over night at Thumb. Weather, clear in the forenoon, cloudy in the afternoon, and a little rain in evening; temperature, mild. Distance, 15 miles.
April 3.—Left Thumb for Snake River Station. Stopped at Lewis River cabin for lunch. Saw signs of 1 elk at Thumb and sign of a moose on Warm Spring Creek, about 2¼ miles from Snake River Station. Weather, cloudy; temperature, mild. Distance, 27 miles.
April 4.—Stayed at Snake River Station. Weather, clear; temperature, mild.
April 5.—Privates Carter, Wharam, and myself left station. Went to Grassy Lake on road that leads to Falls River. Left the road there, turning southwest, coming out in Falls River Basin between Loon Lake and a lake about 2¼ miles south of it, on a creek which has no name. Continued southwest about 3 miles and made a camp. Left Private Wharam in camp and went with Private Carter about 3 miles, coming out in a large flat, which extends northeast and southwest. On southwest end of flat we saw a shack which we went to and found a log honse about 20 by 30 feet. Northwest of house is a log stable about 20 by 50 feet, alongside of which are two large haystacks. South of the house and stable about one-half mile are three stacks more. I believe these are all in the timber reserve about 1½ miles. There were no signs of anyone having been there or around there this winter. The streams in this country are all open, but saw no signs of beaver. Saw 2 mountain lion tracks. After finding cabins and hay Carter and myself returned to camp. Weather, clear; temperature, mild. Distance, 28 miles.
April 6.—Left camp, traveling northwest, striking Falls River near junction of Bechler River; thence up Falls River to Mountain Ash Creek, crossing the river, and up Mountain Ash Creek to cabin on same. Saw fresh signs of moose on Falls River near where we struck it; also fresh sign on Mountain Ash Creek, near cabin. Weather, clear in a. m., cloudy in p. m., snow in evening; temperature, mild. Distance, 22 miles.
April 7.—Left cabin on Mountain Ask Creek for Snake River Station; on arriving there found Scout Whittaker awaiting me with his detachment, having come from Upper Yellowstone. Saw signs of beaver in Proposition Creek. Weather, cloudy and snow; temperature, mild. Distance, 18 miles.
April 8.—Stayed at Snake River Station. Weather, stormy; temperature, mild.
April 9.—Sergeant Leob, Scout Whittaker, Privates Carter, Canivan, and Price, and myself left station, going over Pitchstone Plateau to Shoshone Geyser Basin. In going up Pole Cat Creek saw signs of 6 or 7 elk; sign of 1 in geyser basin. Weather, clear; temperature, mild. Distance, 30 miles.
April 10.—Same party left Shoshone Geyser Basin, going up Shoshone Creek about 3 miles; thence across to Firehole River, down it to Lone Star, there to road ard to

Upper Basin. Saw signs of large game to-day. Weather, clear in forenoon, cloudy in afternoon; temperature, mild. Distance, 15 miles.

April 11.—Same party left Upper Basin, went to Fountain, walking about one-third of the way. Saw trail across road about 4 miles from Upper Basin of buffalo. I think there were 3 of them, but trail was about four days' old and in deep snow, and the number may not be accurate. Many signs of elk between Upper Basin and Fountain. Weather, clear; temperature, mild. Distance, 10 miles.

April 12.—Same party left Fountain for Norris. Saw signs of about 10 elk in Gibbon Canyon. Weather, clear; temperature, mild. Distance, 18 miles.

April 13.—Same party left Norris for Springs. Saw signs of beaver working on Willow Creek. Weather, clear; temperature, mild. Distance, 20 miles.

April 14.—Went to Cinnabar, Mont., to serve subpœnas on James Hawk and Frank Scott. Weather, clear; temperature, mild.

April 15.—Left post for station on Swan Lake Flat. Weather, clear; temperature, mild. Distance, 5 miles.

April 16.—Sergeant Welch, Private Holt, and myself left station, going west on Gardiner River, down it to mouth of Indian Creek, back to station along ridge east of river. The river is open in many places. Some signs of beaver working. Weather, clear; temperature, mild. Distance, 12 miles.

April 17.—Sergeant Welch, Private Holt, and myself left station, going west to Gardiner River, up it about 3 miles, then west across ridge to Fawn Creek, down it to mouth, back to station along ridge east of river. The river is open in many places and much sign of beaver work, one very large dam having been built this spring. Saw 29 elk near mouth of Fawn Creek. Weather, cloudy and snow; temperature, mild. Distance, 19 miles. Left station for post in evening.

April 18.—Remained at post. Weather, clear; temperature, mild.

May 3.—Scout Whittaker and myself left post, going out Cooke City road to Turkey Pen trail, down Blacktail Creek to Yellowstone River, crossing at ford, thence down river to Knowles place, stopping there over night. Examined beaver dams on Blacktail and found them undisturbed. Saw about 350 elk, 8 blacktail, 2 antelope on or near Blacktail. Weather, cloudy; temperature, cold; distance, 14 miles. We left Knowles, going up river to ford. Saw Mike O'Brien near ford fishing. He said he came from Gardiner this a. m. Crossed river, thence up Blacktail Creek to road, and thence to post. Saw about 200 elk, 2 antelope, 2 coyotes, 3 blacktail deer. Weather, cloudy; temperature, cold. Distance, 14 miles.

May 4.—Went part way to Gardiner and back to post on bicycle. Weather, cloudy; temperature, cold.

June 21.—Left post with Private Price for Gallatin; went up Fawn Creek through Fawn Pass; about 3 feet of snow in pass; camped on Gallatin River north of Crowfoot Ridge. Saw 12 elk near head of Fawn Creek; fresh signs of beaver on Fawn Creek opposite pocket. Distance, about 21 miles; weather, clear and warm.

June 22.—Left camp on Gallatin, going down it to where it turns north, then back northeast to head of Stellaria Creek, down to its mouth, and then down Fan Creek to mouth of it, camping on Gallatin River. Saw 1 cow elk on Stellaria Creek; no signs of beaver on any of the streams. Nobody has been in this country this spring. Weather, cloudy and warm. Distance, 14 miles.

June 23.—Leaving the camp on Gallatin, went down the river about 2 miles, when we struck fresh trail of three horses coming up and going back again. Followed trail about 2 miles down Gallatin; there it turned up a small creek coming in from the west; up it about one-half mile found a man in camp, Haskell by name, who had located a mining claim. He is camped about on or near park line (west). Had no horses; said his partner, Curtis, who lives on Gallatin about 3 miles outside of park, had gone to Bozeman for more provisions. Says he has been at his present camp since April 25. Showed us where the cabin was, and I think about one-half of it is in the park. Saw no sign of him doing any trapping or hunting; he had no gun, but plenty of picks and shovels. He is prospecting for George Alderson, of Bozeman. On the 15th he saw 2 men with 2 pack horses and 1 pack mule going up the Gallatin River. Says his partner, Curtis, told him it was "Scotty" and another man from Horr. I followed the trail he showed me up the Gallatin to near the mouth of Fan Creek; there it turned east. Will continue on trail up Fan Creek to-morrow. Saw 1 fish otter in Gallatin River near mouth of Baconrind Creek; while watching him he caught 2 fish. Distance, 17 miles. Weather, cloudy and rainy.

June 24.—Left camp on Gallatin, going up Fan Creek. Saw no signs of trail until I got up about 3 miles, then saw some trail had been made on Gallatin. It made for the pass between Fan Creek and Sportsmans Lake; followed it down Mulharen Creek to park line. Saw signs of fishing in lake. Saw no game to-day. Camped about on north line of park. Weather, cloudy and rainy. Distance, 15 miles.

June 20.—Left post with Privates Wigman and Canivan. Went to Yancey's. Saw no game. Weather, cloudy and rainy. Distance, 20 miles.

July 1.—Left Yancey's, going across bridge of Yellowstone. Camped on river. Saw 9 antelope. Weather, clear. Distance, 8 miles.

July 2.—Left camp on Yellowstone River, going up point of Specimen Ridge and along it to head of Deep Creek. Camped on head of Deep Creek. Saw 29 antelope and 1 elk. Weather, clear. Distance, 18 miles.

July 3.—The 3 pack mules took back trail to Yancey's, Wigman and myself following them, and got them at Yancey's. Stayed there over night, Canivan staying in camp. Saw about 50 antelope on Specimen Ridge. Weather, clear. Distance, 26 miles.

July 4.—Wigman and myself returned to camp on head of Deep Creek. Saw about the same antelope as on 3d. Weather, clear. Distance, 26 miles.

July 5.—Broke camp on Deep Creek, going over Mirror Plateau, crossing head of Opal Creek, then to Timothy, then over to head of Pelican Creek. Camped there. Saw no sign of buffalo. Saw about 5 cow elk with calf and 7 bulls. Distance, 17 miles. Weather, clear.

July 6.—Left the camp on head of Pelican Creek, went west to a small creek that flows into Broad Creek, down it to near its mouth, thence down Broad Creek about 2 miles, thence northeast to hot springs on Shallow Creek, up Shallow Creek to Wapiti Lake, thence east to camp. Saw signs of 3 buffalo (fresh), 2 on the small creek that flows into Broad Creek and one at Wapiti Lake. Saw 15 elk, all cows. Weather, clear. Distance, 15 miles.

July 7.—Left camp on head of Pelican Creek, went down it about 5 miles and made camp. In the afternoon went over to Fern Lake, around it to head of Sour Creek, down it, then followed fresh buffalo trail over ridge to Broad Creek, up it to Fern Lake and on to Tern Lake, from there to camp. Saw one buffalo; jumped 5 buffalo near ford of Broad Creek, following them to Fern Lake, where we saw the one, an old bull, on one of the heads of Sour Creek. Around Ponuntpa Springs there were fresh signs of the band I saw there last winter. I think there are 30 buffalo in this country we came through. Saw about 100 elk. Weather, cloudy and rainy. Distance, 20 miles.

July 8.—Moved camp to Growler, on Plateau Creek. Leaving camp, went up East Fork of Pelican. Saw where 5 or 6 buffalo wintered near forks of Pelican Creek, but no fresh signs. Saw about 150 elk. Weather, clear. Distance, 14 miles.

July 9.—Broke camp and continued down Pelican Creek to the Yellowstone Lake; camped on lake shore about 1 mile from Lake Station. Saw about 100 elk on Pelican, mostly cows with calves, and 16 sand-hill cranes. Weather, clear. Distance, 16 miles.

July 10.—Left camp, going down the Yellowstone River to Canyon; camping there. Saw a black bear on north side of river. Weather, clear. Distance, 18 miles.

July 11.—Went to Norris. Weather, clear. Distance, 11 miles.

July 12.—Went to post. Weather, cloudy and rainy. Distance, 20 miles.

[Fountain Station, 1897.]

November 12.—Holman left station at 8 a. m., crossed the Firehole at footbridge west of the station, followed up Sentinel Creek to its source, and returned to station over same route. Saw tracks of deer and elk. Great many beaver in Sentinel Creek. Distance, 14 miles. Object, scouting.

November 13.—Burdett left station at 8.30 a. m. Followed the road to the Fountain Geyser, from there to Black Warrior, Great Fountain and Excelsior, from there traveled east following a small stream which flows from a basin about 3 miles from Excelsior Basin. Game, tracks of deer and elk.

November 15.—Holman left station at 8 a. m., crossed the Firehole River at wagon bridge which is southwest from the station, followed up Fairy Creek to the falls, and returned to station. Object, to ascertain if any buffalo had crossed going to Hayden Valley. Distance, 9 miles.

November 16.—Holman left station at 8.30 a. m., traveling north. Struck 1 mile west of Gibbon Falls. Followed wagon road to Norris and returned to station. Saw tracks of 1 mountain lion and 3 deer. Object, mail matter. Distance, 35 miles.

November 18.—Holman left station at 8 a. m.; followed trail to Summit Lake cabin, traveled along the west side of Bear Park, and returned to station. Distance, 30 miles.

November 19.—Holman and Burdett left station, 8 a. m., and followed trail to Bear Park; they returned to station, blazing the trail on return trip. Distance, 24 miles. Object, to blaze the trail.

November 23.—Halmon and Stitham left station at 8 a. m., following the road to Firehole Falls; there one man dismounted and followed down the river to its junction with the Gibbon, the other man followed the road, leading one horse. Saw no sign of beaver below the falls; some beaver signs between the falls and the troop camping grounds.

November 24.—Burdett left station 9 a. m.; followed Nez Perce Creek up to the mouth of Magpie; returned to the station over the same route. Distance, 14 miles.
November 27.—Holman left station at 9 a. m., mounted; traveled north and struck Gibbon River below the falls, following down the river on the north side to the junction and then followed the road to the station. Saw some bear signs 1 mile from the junction. Distance, 22 miles.
November 29.—Stitham left station 9 a. m., mounted, following the old road to Mary's Lake and returning to station by the same route. Distance, 20 miles.
November 30.—Burdett left station 9 a. m.; followed wagon road to Norris Station. Object, mail. Distance, 38 miles.
December 3.—Holman and Stitham left station at 7 a. m. on skis. Followed the trail to Summit Lake cabin; arrived there at 7 p. m. The following morning, after putting in wood enough to last one night, we left the cabin and traveled around Bear Park, keeping on the west side. From there we traveled northwest to Lower Bear Park; after scouting through it we returned to station. Saw no sign of buffalo; 15 elk near Twin Buttes, 3 deer near Fairy Falls. Distance traveled, 40 miles. Weather, clear.
December 6.—Mathieson and Stitham left station at 1 p. m. and followed road to Riverside. Stayed there over night and returned to station. Saw several beaver in Madison River; 175 elk in Madison Canyon. Distance, 34 miles. Weather, stormy.
December 10.—Holman and Mathieson left station on skis at 8 a. m. Followed up Nez Perce Creek to Magpie Creek and returned to station. Object, scouting. Distance, 14 miles. Weather, cloudy.
December 11.—Holman and Stitham left station, 8 a. m., on skis. Crossed the Firehole River on the footbridge west of the station; followed up Sentinel Creek to the head of the Queens Laundry and returned to station. Distance, 8 miles. Weather, snowing. Saw tracks of elk.
December 12.—Holman left station at 9 a. m., mounted. Followed the road to Excelsior Geyser. From there traveled southeast to a point 5 miles from Excelsior and returned to station. No sign of game. Distance, 20 miles. Weather, clear.
December 13.—Holman left station at 8 a. m. Traveled southeast to Juniper Creek and returned to station. No sign of game. Distance, 14 miles. Weather, cloudy.
December 14.—Burdett and Mathieson left station at 1 p. m. Traveled southwest to Fairy Falls and returned to station. Transportation, skis. Distance, 8 miles. Weather, clear.
December 17.—Mathieson and Stitham left station 8 a. m., followed old road halfway to Riverside and returned to station. No game. Distance, 17 miles. Weather, cloudy.
December 18.—Holman left station at 8 a. m., mounted. Traveled east to Canyon Creek and returned to station. Distance, 18 miles. No game. Weather, cloudy.
December 21.—Mathieson and Stitham left station, 9 a. m., on skis, followed Nez Perce Creek to foot of Mary's Mountain, and returned to station. Distance, 20 miles. No game. Weather, cloudy.
December 22.—Holman and Stitham left station, 9 a. m., crossed the Firehole River at the footbridge, followed up Sentinel Creek to its source, and returned to station. No game. Distance, 15 miles. Weather, clear.
December 24.—Burdett and Mathieson left station, 1 a. m. Traveled southeast and struck a deep canyon about 5 miles from the station, followed the canyon to the Black Warrior, and followed the wagon road to the station. Saw tracks of 15 elk. Distance, 15 miles. Weather, clear.
December 27.—Mathieson and Stitham left station, 7 a. m.; followed the blazed trail to Summit Lake cabin, stopped there one night, and returned to station. No game. Distance, 30 miles. Stormy scouting.
December 29.—Holman, Mathieson, and Stitham worked at the ice house.
December 30.—Burdett and Stitham left station, 12 m.; followed the Firehole to the falls, and returned to station. Saw some bear tracks across the road. Distance, 10 miles. Weather, clear.

[1898.]

Holman and 4 men worked at ice house from January 3 to January 6, putting up about 20 tons of ice.
January 6.—Holman, Burdett, P., and Burdett, C., left station, 8.15 a. m. Followed the old road to Riverside. Stopped there one night. Holman and Burdett, P., returned to station. Object of trip to accompany Burdett, C., to his station. Distance, 34 miles. Weather, snowing. Saw tracks of 75 elk in Madison Canyon.
January 8.—Mathieson and Stitham left 9 a. m., following down the Firehole to the falls, and returned to station. Saw 25 geese and 40 ducks. Weather, stormy.
January 10.—Holman and 3 men worked at ice house.
January 12.—Burdett, Mathieson, and Stitham left station at 9 a. m., crossed the

YELLOWSTONE NATIONAL PARK.

Firehole River, at the first bridge, followed up Sentinel Creek to the beaver dams, and returned to station. Saw 12 geese, 25 ducks, and 1 swan. Distance, 10 miles.

January 13.—Holman, Burdett, and Mathieson left station 8.30 a. m; followed Nez Perce Creek to the foot of Mary's Mountain, and returned to station. Saw 1 beaver, 3 elk, and 19 ducks. Tracks of 50 elk. Distance, 20 miles. Weather, snowy.

January 14.—Holman and Stitham left station at 11 a. m; followed the road to Canyon Creek, and returned to station. Saw 12 ducks. Lieutenant Lindsley and Scout Morrison arrived from Riverside.

January 15.—Mathieson left the station at 8 a. m. and followed the telegraph line to Canyon Creek, where he met Private Holt, who was ordered here from Norris, and returned to station. Distance, 18 miles. Weather, clear.

January 16.—Lieutenant Lindsley and detachment left for Snake River via Upper Basin and Thumb, taking 2 men, mounted, from here, as far as the Upper Basin, with rations.

January 17.—Burdett and Mathieson returned from Upper Basin. Saw 50 ducks on Firehole River. Weather, cloudy.

January 18.—Mathieson and Syberty left station at 8 a. m. on skis; traveled northeast, and struck Magpie Creek about 4 miles from its mouth; followed this stream to its junction with the Nez Perce, thence west along the Nez Perce to the station. Saw 3 elk. Weather, clear; distance, 18 miles.

January 19.—Holman and Burdett left station 9 a. m. on skis; followed the road to Norris Station, remained there one day, and returned to station on the 21st. Object, mail.

January 24.—Holman, Burdett, and Mathieson left station at 7 a. m. and followed the road to the Upper Basin; stayed there one night, and left the next day at 7 a. m.; scouted through the Black Sand and Biscuit basins, and returned to station. Weather, clear; distance traveled, about 30 miles.

January 28.—Holman, Burdett, and Syberty left station 1 p. m.; crossed the Firehole River at the footbridge and followed Sentinel Creek to the Queen's Laundry, thence south to Twin Buttes, thence east to the river, and followed the river to the station. Distance, 10 miles. One hundred ducks in the river. Weather, clear.

January 31.—Holman, Burdett, and Mathieson left station at 8 a. m.; followed up Nez Perce Creek to the mouth of Juniper Creek, and then followed up Juniper to the hot springs, thence east to Spruce Creek and down Spruce to its junction with the Nez Perce, thence west along the Nez Perce to the station. Saw tracks of 10 elk and some beaver signs in Spruce Creek; also saw a great number of geese, ducks and fishes in and along the streams. Distance traveled, about 20 miles. Weather, fine.

February 2.—Burdett and Syberty left station at 8 a. m.; followed the road to Canyon Creek, and returned to station. Object, breaking trail.

February 3.—Burdett and Syberty left station at 7 a. m. on skis; followed the old road to the foot of Mary's Mountain, and returned to station. Object, to meet Holt and Stitham, who were coming in from Mud Geyser. Weather, snowy.

February 6.—Holman, Burdett, and Syberty left station at 9 a. m. mounted; followed the road to Madison Canyon, and returned. Saw tracks of 100 elk. Distance, 16 miles. Weather, stormy.

February 7.—Stitham and Syberty left station at 8 a. m.; followed road to Canyon Creek, and returned to station. Object, breaking trail. Cloudy.

February 8.—Holman, Burdett, and Syberty left station at 8 a. m.; followed up Nez Perce Creek to the mouth of Magpie Creek, thence north along Magpie to a point 5 miles from its mouth, and returned to station over the same route. Saw tracks of 5 elk. Distance, 20 miles. Object, scouting.

February 9.—Holman, Burdett, and Syberty left station at 9 a. m., following the old road to Mary's Lake. After scouting along the foot of the mountain two hours, we returned to the station. Saw 20 elk. Distance, 24 miles. Cloudy.

February 10.—Holman, Burdett, and Syberty left station at 7 a. m. on skis; followed up Nez Perce Creek to the mouth of Spruce Creek, thence up Spruce Creek to the hot springs, and returned to station. Saw tracks of 10 elk. Distance, 24 miles. Weather, fine.

February 14.—Holman, Burdett, and Stitham left station at 7 a. m.; followed the trail to Summit Lake cabin, arrived there at 5 p. m. Saw 1 swan and tracks of 5 elk between the station and Twin Buttes. Distance, 15 miles. Weather, stormy.

February 15.—Left Summit Lake cabin at 9 a. m.; traveled south to Summit Lake, thence west to hot springs and then back to the lake, thence south to hot springs, 1 mile south of the lake, and then followed the trail back to the cabin. Saw tracks of 1 mountain lion. Distance, 10 miles. Weather, stormy.

February 16.—Left the cabin at 9 a. m., went northwest to Lower Bear Park, from here followed the trail to the station. Saw tracks of 10 elk near Twin Buttes. Distance, 15 miles. Weather, snowy. Object, scouting.

February 22.—Holman, Burdette, and Syberty left station at 9 a. m. with five day's

88   YELLOWSTONE NATIONAL PARK.

rations; followed the road to the Upper Basin; stayed there until the following morning; left there at 8 o'clock; followed the road to the Lone Star Geyser; there we took off our skis and waded the Firehole River and followed it to a point about 3 miles north of Madison Lake. Here we left the river and traveled southeast and struck Shoshone Creek 2 or 3 miles from the Shoshone Geyser Basin, where we made camp. Left Shoshone Creek the following morning; followed down the creek to the lake, and followed around on the side of the lake. Made camp on Heron Creek; left Heron Creek the next morning at daylight and struck the main road near the 9-mile post; followed it to the Upper Basin station and stayed there for the night. Left the Upper Basin the next morning and followed the road to the station. Saw 10 elk near Twin Buttes, tracks of 2 elk near the station. Saw no sign of game in Shoshone Basin. Distance traveled, about 67 miles. Weather, cloudy and snowing.

March 2.—Burdett, Mathieson, and Syberty left station at 9 a. m; followed up the Firehole River to the Biscuit Basin and returned to station via Great Fountain Geyser. Saw tracks of 15 elk. Weather, clear.

March 3.—Holman left station mounted, and followed up Nez Perce Creek to the foot of Mary's Mountain and returned to station. Saw tracks of 25 elk near the mountain. Saw 25 elk 2 miles from the station.

March 4.—Burdett, Mathieson, and Syberty left station at 8 a. m. and followed the road to the junction of the Firehole and Gibbon rivers; from there, followed up the Gibbon to a point about 5 miles from the falls and returned to station over the same route. Saw 200 elk near the junction of the rivers, and saw tracks of a great many elk. Distance, 24 miles.

March 10.—Holman, Burdett, and Mathieson left station at 8 a. m; followed the road to Norris, remained there one day, and left Norris on the morning of the 12th; followed the wagon road to the post; remained at the post two days to draw clothing. Holman and Burdett left the post on the morning of the 15th; followed the road to Crystal Springs, stopped there one night; on the following day followed the road to Norris; left Norris next morning and followed the road to the station. Distance traveled, 78 miles. Object, to accompany Mathieson to the post on account of expiration of his term of service.

March 19.—Holman and Syberty left station on skis; followed the road to the Upper Basin, stopped there overnight, and returned to station via Biscuit Basin. No game. Weather, snowing.

March 23.—Left station with one man, crossed the river on the foot bridge, followed up Sentinel Creek to the head of the Queen's Laundry, and returned to station.

March 26.—Holman and Syberty left station at 7 a. m.; followed the road to the junction of the Firehole and Gibbon rivers; from there followed up on the north side of Gibbon River to near the falls; crossed the river and followed the road to the 9-mile post from the hotel; left the road there, traveled south and struck the telegraph line and followed it to the station. Saw 15 elk along the Gibbon River. Saw tracks of 250 elk. Distance traveled, 22 miles. Weather, snowing.

March 29.—Holman, Stitham, and Syberty left at 6.30 a. m.; followed up Nez Perce Creek to the foot of Mary's Mountain; from there followed up a small stream that flows southward along the mountain to a point about 3 miles from its mouth; thence west to Magpie Creek, and then down Magpie to the road and followed the road to the station. Saw 1 elk and tracks of 15. Some fresh beaver signs in a small stream near the mountain. Distance traveled, 20 miles. Weather, fine. Object, scouting.

March 30.—Holman, Stitham, and Syberty left station at 7 a. m.; traveled southeast and came to a deep canyon about 4 miles from the station; followed down the canyon to the Black Warrior; from there traveled around the Great Fountain and near to the Excelsior, and followed the road to the station. Saw tracks of 3 elk near the station. Saw a stray horse at the Black Warrior. Distance, 12 miles. Weather, snowy.

April 2.—Stitham and Syberty left station 6 a. m.; followed the road to Norris station; there one night and returned to station. Object, mail.

April 5.—Holman, Stitham, and Syberty left station at 6.15 a. m; followed up Nez Perce Creek to Spruce Creek, thence up Spruce to the hot springs, thence north along the mountain to the old road, thence west to the station. Saw tracks of 25 elk; saw 2 coyotes and 1 red fox. Distance, 24 miles. Weather, fine.

April 8.—Holman, Stitham, and Syberty left station at 7 a. m. on skis; traveled southwest to Twin Buttes, thence northwest to the head of the Queen's Laundry, thence east to the station. Saw 7 elk near Twin Buttes; 5 coyotes; tracks of 10 elk. Distance, 10 miles. Weather, fine.

April 12.—Stitham and Syberty left station at 4.30 a. m.; followed up the road and struck buffalo trail 4 miles north of Upper Basin; followed trail up for 4 or 5 miles; lost the trail there, and then traveled south to the Upper Basin; stopped there for the night and returned to station the next day. Distance traveled, 30 miles.

April 14.—Holman and Syberty left station at 6 a. m., on skis; followed the road to Madison Canyon; from there followed up the Gibbon River for about 5 miles, then returned to station. Saw 40 elk and tracks of 200, 2 minks and 3 muskrats in the Firehole, 2 coyotes, and 1 red fox. Distance traveled, 24 miles. Weather, fine. From all indications the elk are leaving Madison Canyon and coming into the Lower Basin.

April 15.—Stitham and Syberty left station on skis at 5.30 a. m.; followed the road to Canyon Creek and returned to station. Saw tracks of 1 bear. Weather, fine. Distance, 18 miles. Object, mail.

April 16.—Holman left station at 8 a. m., mounted; followed Nez Perce Creek to the mountain and then traveled south along Mary's Mountain; struck Spruce Creek about 5 miles from its mouth and followed it to the Nez Perce, then followed it to the station. Saw tracks of 75 elk. Saw 1 red fox and 2 coyotes. Weather, fine. Distance traveled, 22 miles. Object, scouting. A great many fresh beaver signs along the Nez Perce.

April 17.—Stitham and Syberty left station, mounted, at 1 p. m.; followed the road to Madison Canyon; there they met Sergeant Bernstein and 2 men from Riverside. They stopped there one hour and returned to station. Saw tracks of 20 elk. Distance traveled, 16 miles. Weather, snowing. Object, to take some packages for Sergeant Bernstein which had been left here.

April 18.—Holman and Syberty left station at 8 a. m.; followed the road to first bridge south of the Excelsior; there we left the road and patrolled through the Biscuit Basin. Arrived at the Upper Basin at 12 m.; stopped there one hour for lunch, and then followed the road down to the 5-mile post; left the road and followed up a small stream which flows from a hot basin. Patrolled all through the basin and returned to station. Saw tracks of 15 elk. Saw 2 coyotes. Distance traveled, about 35 miles. Weather, fine.

April 19.—Stitham and Ornes left station at 12 m. and followed the road to Riverside. Stitham stopped there one night and returned to station. Object of trip, to take Ornes to Riverside. He came out here on skis and was ordered to go to Riverside; as the snow is nearly all gone, he couldn't go on skis, and I sent him down mounted.

April 21.—Stitham and Syberty left station, mounted, at 10 a. m.; followed the road to Norris, and arrived there at 3 p. m. Returned to station the following morning. Saw tracks of 23 elk. Saw 1 bear and 3 cubs. Distance traveled, 38 miles. Weather, snowing. Object, mail.

April 23.—Holman left station at 9 a. m.; followed Sentinel Creek to the beaver dams and returned to station. Saw tracks of about 30 elk. Distance traveled, 8 miles. Weather, clear. Object, to look after the beaver.

April 24.—Holman left station at 8 a. m., mounted; followed the road to Riverside Station; there three hours and returned to station. Saw 2 coyotes, 3 muskrats, 1 mink, 1 badger, 2 grouse, tracks of 8 elk, and some fresh beaver signs along the Firehole. Met Scout Whittaker on the road to Riverside with pack train. Object, a trip to take some mail to Riverside and to get some fresh meat. Distance, 34 miles. Weather, fine.

April 25.—Holman left station, dismounted, at 8 a. m.; followed up Nez Perce Creek to Magpie; waded all through the beaver dams and returned to station. Saw 1 coyote, tracks of 30 elk, 3 sand-hill cranes. Distance, 10 miles. Weather, fine.

April 26.—Holman left station at 7 a. m., dismounted; traveled southwest to Twin Buttes and returned to station. Saw 39 elk, 2 coyotes, 4 sand-hill cranes, and 1 mink. Distance traveled, 10 miles. Weather, clear and high winds. Object of the trip, to try the skis between Twin Buttes and Summit Lake Cabin.

April 27.—Burdett and Stitham left station at 10 a. m. to go to the post, in compliance with verbal orders from the commanding officer.

April 28.—Syberty left station at 7 a. m., mounted, following the road to the post; remained there one day and returned to Norris on the 30th. Left Norris on the 1st of May and came back to station by the road. Distance traveled, 78 miles. Object, to get the horses shod.

May 3.—Holman left station, mounted; followed the old road half way to Riverside and returned to station. Saw 1 mink, 1 coyote, and tracks of 15 elk. Distance traveled, 16 miles. Weather, cloudy. Object, scouting.

May 4.—Holman left station at 9 a. m.; followed the road to the Upper Basin, mounted, and returned to station. Saw 81 elk and 1 coyote, and 4 sand-hill cranes. Distance traveled, 20 miles. Weather, cloudy. Object, scouting.

May 5.—Holman left station at 9 a. m., mounted; followed up Nez Perce Creek to the foot of Mary's Mountain and returned to station. Saw 1 coyote, 1 mink, 2 sand-hill cranes, and tracks of 75 elk. Distance traveled, 16 miles. Weather, snowing. Object, scouting.

May 6.—Holman left station at 9 a. m., crossed the Firehole River on footbridge west of the station, struck Sentinel Creek near its mouth, followed it to the head of the Queen's Laundry, and returned to station. Saw 1 bear, 1 mink, tracks of 15 elk.

Distance, 8 miles. Weather, clear. Object, scouting. Transportation, dismounted (on foot).

May 7.—Holman left station at 7.30 a. m., dismounted, to look for the horses which have strayed away. Struck their trail on the road leading to Norris; followed the trail up to Gibbon Canyon; there I met the lineman. He said he saw 2 horses in Elk Park; followed the road to Elk Park, looked all down the park, but did not find them; followed the road to Norris. Moore went out mounted, and found them near the station. I remained there until 3 p. m. and returned to the station. Distance traveled, about 45 miles. Weather, cloudy. Saw 1 mink in the Gibbon, tracks of 1 bear, and about 7 elk.

May 8.—Syberty left station, mounted, at 8 a. m.; followed the road to Norris and returned to station on the 9th. Distance traveled, 38 miles. Weather, clear. Object, mail.

May 10.—Holman left station at 7 a. m., followed the road to the post, remained there two days, left the post on the 14th, followed the road to Norris, stayed there one night, and came to the station on the 15th. Distance traveled, 78 miles.

May 18.—Holman left station at 9.30 a. m., mounted, for Riverside Station; arrived there at 1 p. m. Saw 15 elk, 7 badgers, 1 coyote, 2 grouse, and tracks of 1 bear. Weather, raining. Left on the morning of the 19th, followed the road to the station; saw numerous geese and 1 pheasant. Distance traveled, 32 miles. Syberty left station at 10 a. m., mounted; followed up the road to the Biscuit Basin, patrolled through the basin and returned to station. Saw 4 blacktail deer, 2 bear, 1 silver fox, and numerous geese. Distance traveled, 15 miles. Weather, snowing and blowing.

May 20.—Syberty patrolled road to Madison Canyon and return. Saw 18 antelope near Gibbon Bridge; tracks of 11 elk. Distance traveled, 16 miles. Weather, cloudy and snowing. Holman left station, mounted, at 10 a. m.; followed up Nez Perce Creek to the mouth of Magpie Creek, waded all through the beaver dams, found everything O. K., and returned to station. Saw 1 coyote, 2 minks, 2 grouse, and numerous geese. Distance traveled, 10 miles.

May 23.—Holman left station, mounted, at 10 a. m.; crossed the Firehole River at ford, followed up Sentinel Creek to the head of the Queen's Laundry, examined the beaver dams closely, and returned to station. Saw 75 elk, 1 coyote, numerous geese and ducks. Distance traveled, 8 miles. Weather, rainy. Object, scouting.

May 24.—Holman and Syberty left station at 7.30 a. m., mounted, following up the road to the Lone Star Geyser. Then we dismounted and tied our horses up and followed up the Firehole River to a point about 3 miles south of the Lone Star. Looked closely for beaver signs, but found no fresh ones. Returned to station at 5.30 p. m. Saw 1 bear, 1 coyote, tracks of 30 or 40 elk. Distance traveled, 34 miles. Weather, rainy. Object, scouting.

May 25.—Holman left station, mounted, at 1 p. m.; followed up Nez Perce Creek to the mouth of Magpie and returned to station. Saw tracks of 19 elk and of 1 bear. Distance traveled, 10 miles. Weather, cloudy. Object, scouting.

May 26.—Syberty left station at 8 a. m.; followed the road to Riverside, remained there one night and returned to the station the following day. Saw numerous geese. Distance, 32 miles. Weather, cloudy.

May 29.—Holman left, mounted, at 1 p. m.; traveled southeast to Twin Buttes and returned to station. Saw 27 elk, 1 coyote, 2 grouse, tracks of 1 bear. Weather, cloudy.

DEPARTMENT OF JUSTICE,
Washington, D. C., November 17, 1898.

The SECRETARY OF THE INTERIOR.

SIR: Section 5388 of the Revised Statutes, as amended by the act of June 4, 1888 (25 Stat., 166), provides as follows:

Every person who unlawfully cuts, or aids, or is employed in unlawfully cutting, or wantonly destroys, or procures to be wantonly destroyed, any timber standing upon the land of the United States which, in pursuance of law, may be reserved or purchased for military or other purposes, or upon any Indian reservation or lands belonging to or occupied by any tribe of Indians under authority of the United States, shall pay a fine of not more than five hundred dollars or be imprisoned not more than twelve months, or both, in the discretion of the court.

The act of June 4, 1897, entitled, "An act making appropriations for sundry civil expenses of the Government for the fiscal year ending June 30, 1896, and for other purposes," provides (28 Stat., 35):

The Secretary of the Interior shall make provisions for the protection against destruction by fire and depredations upon the public forests and forest reservations which may have been set aside or which may be hereafter set aside under the said act of March 3, 1891, and which may be continued; and he may make such rules and regulations and establish such service as will insure the objects of such reservations, namely, to regulate their occupancy and use and to preserve the forests thereon from destruction; and any violation of the provisions of this act or such rules and regulations shall be punished as is provided for in the act of June 4, 1888, amending section 5388 of the Revised Statutes of the United States.

Under the authority thus conferred the Secretary of the Interior, on June 30, 1897, promulgated certain rules and regulations for the purpose of regulating the occupancy and use of the forest reservations and to preserve the forests thereon from destruction, among which was the following:

13. The pasturing of live stock on the public lands in forest reservations will not be interfered with so long as it appears that injury is not being done to the forest growth and the rights of others are not thereby jeopardized. The pasturing of sheep is, however, prohibited in all forest reservations, except those in the States of Oregon and Washington, for the reason that sheep grazing has been found injurious to the forest cover, and therefore of serious consequence in regions where the rainfall is limited. The exception in favor of the States of Oregon and Washington is made because the continuous moisture and abundant rainfall of the Cascade and Pacific coast ranges make rapid renewal of herbage and undergrowth possible, etc.

In view of the foregoing, you request my opinion whether a criminal prosecution will lie to punish a person who grazes sheep in a forest reservation in violation of the regulation quoted.

I recognize the existence of the salutary rule that Congress can not delegate its legislative power so as to authorize an administrative officer, by the adoption of regulations, to create an offense and prescribe its punishment. But here the statute proclaims the punishment for an offense which, in general terms, is defined by law, the regulation dealing only with a matter of detail and administration necessary to carry into effect the object of the law. The protection of the public forests is intrusted to the Secretary of the Interior. Section 5388 makes it an offense, punishable by fine and imprisonment, for any person wantonly to destroy any timber on a public reservation. In furtherance of this policy, the act of June 4, 1897, directs the Secretary to make provision for the protection of the forests and authorizes him to regulate the use and occupancy of the forest reservations and to preserve the forests thereon from destruction, making for such purpose proper rules and regulations. Any violation of such rules and regulations is, by the statute, made an offense, punishable as provided in section 5388.

By this law the control of the occupancy and use of these reservations is handed over to the Secretary for the purpose of preserving the forests thereon, and any occupancy or use in violation of the rules and regulations adopted by him is made punishable criminally. It seems to me Congress has a right to do this. Suppose Congress had provided that the occupation or use of a forest reservation by any person, without permission of the Secretary, should be a misdemeanor? Would not this be a valid exercise of legislative power? The present statute does no more. The regulation is reasonable and necessary. It restrains no one in the enjoyment of any natural or legal right. To use the language of Mr. Chief Justice Fuller in In re Kollock (165 U. S., 526, 533):

> The regulation was in execution of, or supplementary to, but not in conflict with, the law itself, and was specifically authorized thereby in effectuation of the legislation which created the offense.

Your question, therefore, is answered in the affirmative.

Very respectfully,

JOHN K. RICHARDS, *Solicitor-General.*

Approved.

JOHN W. GRIGGS, *Attorney-General.*

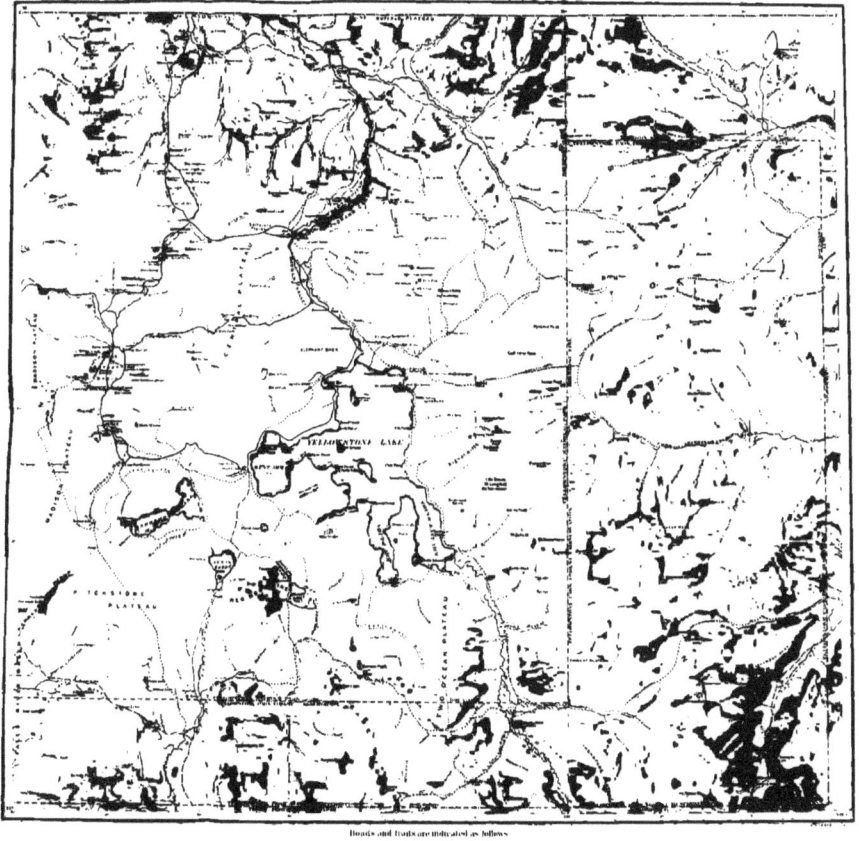

www.ingramcontent.com/pod-product-compliance
Lightning Source LLC
Chambersburg PA
CBHW032246080426
42735CB00008B/1023